THE CONDUCT OF BRITISH EMPIRE FOREIGN RELATIONS SINCE THE PEACE SETTLEMENT

THE CONDUCT OF BRITISH EMPIRE FOREIGN RELATIONS SINCE THE PEACE SETTLEMENT

BY

ARNOLD J. TOYNBEE

*Director of Studies in the Royal Institute
of International Affairs
Research Professor of International History
in the University of London
(both on the Sir Daniel Stevenson Foundation)*

Tu tecum imperio populos sociare memento.
Hae tibi erunt artes: exemplo pandere mores.
Ducere tranquillos et conciliare rebelles.

OXFORD UNIVERSITY PRESS
LONDON: HUMPHREY MILFORD

*Issued under the auspices of the Royal Institute of
International Affairs*

1928

OXFORD
UNIVERSITY PRESS
LONDON: AMEN HOUSE, E.C.4
EDINBURGH GLASGOW LEIPZIG
COPENHAGEN NEW YORK TORONTO
MELBOURNE CAPETOWN BOMBAY
CALCUTTA MADRAS SHANGHAI
HUMPHREY MILFORD
PUBLISHER TO THE
UNIVERSITY

Printed in Great Britain

PREFACE

PROFESSOR TOYNBEE's explanation in his prefatory note of the scope of this little volume gives the reason for the decision to publish it as a separate work, distinct from, though supplementary to, the regular *Survey* volumes. It is hoped that the great interest attaching to the recent developments that Professor Toynbee so ably sketches will ensure for the volume a warm welcome both in this country and in the Dominions.

G. M. GATHORNE-HARDY.

NOTE BY THE WRITER

THIS small volume has been given a long and rather clumsy title in order to show clearly what ground it does and what it does not attempt to cover. In the first place, it does not attempt to give a record of what the foreign relations of the British Empire were during the years in question. During those years, as is pointed out on p. 4, the foreign relations of the Empire were almost coextensive with the entire field of international affairs, which is the subject of the annual volumes of the *Survey*. The scope of the present volume is restricted to the consideration of how these foreign relations of the British Empire were conducted during a period when the arrangements for the conduct of them were changing and growing very rapidly. In other words, this volume is concerned not so much with political as with constitutional history; and, here again, it is only one aspect of constitutional history that is in question—the aspect that bears upon foreign, as distinct from inter-imperial or internal, affairs. The constitutional history of inter-imperial relations has only been touched upon in so far as this has seemed necessary in order to throw light on certain problems and controversies which arose over the conduct of foreign relations.

It is true that these two aspects of the constitutional history of the British Empire cannot be isolated from one another completely; and this is especially true of a period in which the conduct of British Empire foreign relations ceased to be centralized in Whitehall. The special interest of this period lies, of course, in the fact that, in the course of it, the self-governing Members of the British Commonwealth overseas, in full agreement with His Majesty's Government in Great Britain, began to enter into direct relations with foreign Governments in the political as well as in the economic sphere, in contrast to their previous practice of leaving political relations to be dealt with by the Foreign Office and its representatives in foreign capitals. The crux of this new development in the conduct of British Empire foreign relations was the problem of co-ordination, and it is evident that this cannot be dealt with without entering into the question of inter-imperial relations rather deeply.

At the same time, it may be well to note that any attempt to deal with inter-imperial affairs comprehensively has been deliberately avoided in this volume, and that it has proved possible to leave the greater part of that vast field out of the discussion altogether. A comprehensive treatment of inter-imperial affairs since the Peace Settlement would mean giving a complete record of the evolution of the British Commonwealth within the British Empire, through the development of Dominion status, during the years in question; and it may not be out of place to indicate here very briefly some of the topics which such a record would have to cover.

A first topic would be the political relations between States Members of the Commonwealth; and this would include the proceedings of the three

Imperial Conferences of 1921, 1923, and 1926, the steps taken towards solving the problem of the permanent representation of States Members of the Commonwealth in one another's capitals; and the history of the establishment of the Dominions Office in Whitehall and of corresponding departments in the capitals of other States Members of the Commonwealth (for example, New Zealand).

A second topic would be the constitutional and legal relations between States Members of the Commonwealth; and this would involve dealing with the official adoption of the term 'Commonwealth' in 1921, with the change in the title of His Majesty the King in 1926, with the metamorphosis of the office of Governor-General, with the operation of Westminster legislation in the Dominions and of Dominion legislation in other parts of the Empire, with merchant shipping legislation, with appeals from the Dominions to the Judicial Committee of the Privy Council in London, and with the Flag Question in the Dominions, particularly in the Union of South Africa.

A third topic would be the social and economic relations between States Members of the Commonwealth: for example, the provision of special facilities on the London Money Market for Overseas Members, the whole subject of fiscal relations (as illustrated by Dominion and Indian preferences and excises), the economic development of the Dominions, and the organization and control of immigration into their territories both from Great Britain and Ireland and from foreign countries.

A fourth topic would be the progress of certain communities in the Empire towards Dominion Status; and here it would be necessary to record the creation of a new self-governing Dominion through the establishment of the Irish Free State, the evolution of a new self-governing Dominion through the working of the Government of India Act of 1919, and a number of changes in the status and constitution of certain non-self-governing colonies and protectorates. This last head would include such events as the erection of Southern Rhodesia into a self-governing colony, the introduction of 'dyarchy' into the government of Malta, the conflict between British colonial administration and Greek nationalism in Cyprus, the grant of majorities of elected members in colonial councils and assemblies (for instance, in Ceylon), and the work of constitutional reorganization in the Federated Malay States.

A fifth topic would be the history of territorial questions: for example, the settlement of the Labrador Boundary Question and the deferment of the attempt to arrive at a definite settlement of the Irish Boundary Question.

A sixth topic would be a survey of schemes for local associations within the Empire, as illustrated by the negotiations between the Union of South Africa and Southern Rhodesia for the entry of Southern Rhodesia into the Union, by the suggestion for the eventual entry into the Union of South Africa of the mandated territory of South West Africa (a suggestion which threatened to raise a formidable problem in international law), by the project of a British East African Federation which was investigated on the spot by a Royal Commission in 1928, and by the inauguration of a periodical West Indian Conference in 1925.

A seventh topic would be the development of cultural and racial relations within the Empire, and this would involve a survey of the status of Indians in various communities of the Empire outside India and a survey of the situation of the native populations in various parts of British Africa.

An eighth topic would be the economic development of the Colonial Empire (as distinguished from the group of States Members of the Commonwealth), with a record of the proceedings of the Economic Conference of 1923 and the Colonial Conference of 1927.

A ninth topic would be the opening up of British Imperial Airways.

A tenth topic would be Imperial Defence: the co-operation between Great Britain and other States Members of the Commonwealth in constructing the Singapore Naval Base and other naval and military works, the development of Dominion Navies, the Indianization of the Indian Army, and the co-ordinating activities of the Committee of Imperial Defence on sea and land and in the air. Since the existence of a problem of Imperial Defence implies relations between the British Empire and foreign Powers, this would be the point at which a survey of inter-Imperial relations would merge into a survey of British Empire foreign relations.

It will be seen, from this very brief review, that the inter-Imperial relations alone of the British Empire were comparable, in their multiplicity and their complexity, to the international relations of the world at large. A complete record of them might fill almost as many pages as a Survey of International Affairs.

A. J. T.

Note—The writer has unfortunately been unable to make use of Dr. K. Heck's 'Der Aufbau des britischen Reiches', which did not come into his hands until the present volume was in the press. Dr. Heck's book (published, as Heft 3 in the series *Beiträge zum ausländischen öffentlichen Recht und Völkerrecht, herausgegeben vom Institut für ausländisches öffentliches Recht und Völkerrecht in Berlin*, by de Gruyter, Berlin and Leipzig, 1927) is an introduction to and commentary on the British Parliamentary Paper *Cmd.* 2768 of 1926.

CONTENTS

INTRODUCTION 1

(i) BRITISH CITIZENSHIP: DISTINCTIONS DRAWN BETWEEN DIF-
FERENT CATEGORIES OF BRITISH CITIZENS BY FOREIGN GOVERN-
MENTS

    (a) The exclusion, by United States Legislation, of British
Subjects of certain Races and Provenances from Immigration into the United States 44

    (b) The Privileged Status, under the United States Immigra-
tion Act of 1924, of British Citizens of Canadian Birth . 45

(ii) THE DISTINCTION BETWEEN 'PASSIVE' AND 'ACTIVE' BELLI-
GERENCY: THE 'CHANĀQ INCIDENT' OF SEPTEMBER 1922 . 46

(iii) THE MEMBERSHIP IN THE LEAGUE OF NATIONS OF STATES MEM-
BERS OF THE BRITISH COMMONWEALTH 52

    (a) The Admission of the Irish Free State . . . 53

    (b) The Registration at Geneva of the Articles of Agreement
of the 6th December, 1921, by the Government of the Irish
Free State 54

    (c) The Action taken by Canada with a view to the Modifica-
tion of Article 10 of the Covenant 56

    (d) The Candidature of the Irish Free State (1926) and the
Election of Canada (1927) to a Temporary Seat on the
League Council 58

    (e) The Exercise of League Mandates by South Africa,
Australia, and New Zealand, as well as by the British
Empire 60

(iv) THE DIPLOMATIC AND CONSULAR REPRESENTATION OF STATES
MEMBERS OF THE BRITISH COMMONWEALTH (OTHER THAN
GREAT BRITAIN) AND OF FOREIGN STATES IN ONE ANOTHER'S
CAPITALS

    (a) The U.S.-Canadian International Joint Commission . 61

    (b) The Diplomatic Representation of Canada in Washington
and of the United States at Ottawa 64

    (c) The Diplomatic Representation of the Irish Free State in
Washington 67

    (d) The Issue of Exequaturs to Foreign Consuls in the
Dominions 71

(v) CO-OPERATION BETWEEN STATES MEMBERS OF THE COMMON-
WEALTH IN THE CONDUCT OF FOREIGN RELATIONS

    (a) The Personal Contact between Prime Ministers in the

CONTENTS

Imperial Conferences of 1921, 1923, and 1926, and the Supplementation of this by other Methods of Communication and Consultation 72

(b) The Representation of the British Empire at International Conferences (1919–26) and the Obligations of States Members of the Commonwealth in regard to Treaties resulting therefrom 83

(c) The Negotiation, Signature and Ratification of International Treaties and Agreements not issuing out of International Conferences 99

APPENDIX

FRONTIER RELATIONS BETWEEN CANADA AND THE UNITED STATES

(a) Water Questions arising in the Basin of the St. Lawrence and the Great Lakes 111

(b) The Smuggling Problem 117

INDEX 121

THE CONDUCT OF BRITISH EMPIRE FOREIGN RELATIONS SINCE THE PEACE SETTLEMENT

Introduction.

ON the 19th November, 1926, the Imperial Conference then sitting in London unanimously adopted a report from their Committee on Inter-Imperial Relations in which it was pronounced that the British Empire, ' considered as a whole, defies classification and bears no real resemblance to any other political organization which now exists or has ever yet been tried '. This Committee, which sat under the chairmanship of Lord Balfour, included nine other distinguished statesmen who were at that time Ministers of the Crown, among them the Prime Ministers of the four senior self-governing Dominions. An historian, confronted with a pronouncement of so unquestionable an authority and so formidable a purport, is reduced to approaching the British Empire, as Herodotus approached Egypt, under cover of a series of paradoxes.

The fundamental paradox of this mysterious ' political organization ' was its simultaneous unity and multiplicity. On the one hand, the British Empire was undoubtedly a single state in both municipal and international law. In municipal law this unity was signified by the existence of a common British citizenship consisting in the uniform allegiance of ' subjects ' to a single crown—a bond which made it impossible, so long as the Empire existed, for any one community of ' British subjects ' to go to war with any other, however fully such communities might be endowed, in other respects, with the attributes of sovereign independent states. Conversely, it was impossible for any community of ' British subjects ' to be at peace with a foreign country with which the British Empire was at war or to be at war with a country with which the Empire was at peace [1]— a solidarity in belligerency and neutrality which signified the unity

---

[1] This proposition was denied, at least in principle, by General Hertzog in a statement which he read to the House of Assembly at Pretoria on the 8th March, 1928, in presenting for the approval of the House the Report of the Inter-Imperial Relations Committee which had been adopted by the Imperial Conference of 1926. In this statement General Hertzog contended that Dominion status, as now recognized, implied a right to remain neutral if Great Britain went to war. In answer to a question in the House, General Hertzog stated that this question of neutrality had not been discussed by the Imperial Conference itself (*The Times*, 9th March, 1928. The full text of the speech is printed in *The Cape Times* and other South African papers for the 9th March, 1928).

of the Empire in international law in a most emphatic manner.   In this connexion it may be noted that, in the successive international negotiations for the establishment of agreed ratios of naval strength, from the Washington Conference onwards, it appears to have been taken for granted that the British Empire should be treated as a single unit in relation to other naval Powers.   Yet this was by no means the end of the matter, for, on the other hand, the unity of British citizenship was disregarded, in certain particulars, not only by foreign Governments but by Governments of states members of the British Commonwealth ; [1] and the solidarity of British belligerency was qualified by the doctrine (which had been accepted explicitly as between the states members of the Commonwealth themselves) that the belligerency to which a self-governing community in the British Empire stood committed automatically, if and when the Empire found itself at war, was a ' passive ' belligerency only, since in ' active ' belligerency, as in other positive activities of state, ' every Dominion is now, and must always remain, the sole judge of the nature and extent of its co-operation '.[2]

This doctrine, thus authoritatively formulated in 1926, had already been established empirically by a number of striking precedents on important occasions.   Even in the short period which had elapsed since the coming into force of the Versailles Treaty at the beginning of 1920, the validity of the distinction between ' passive ' and

[1] The United States Immigration Laws excluded British subjects of certain races, who hailed from certain regions, from immigration into the United States, while they admitted British subjects of other races on the quota system.   Again, they gave a privileged status, in the matter of immigration, to any British subjects belonging to the non-excluded races who happened to have been born in Canada.   These were distinctions of which British law in Great Britain was not cognizant.   On the other hand, certain self-governing communities of British subjects gave differential treatment on similar lines, in this same matter of immigration, to their fellow subjects according to categories which the Governments of these self-governing communities established for their own purposes at their own discretion (see *Survey for 1924*, pp. 130 and 141–2).   Even before the General War of 1914–18 Canada had found herself under the necessity of making a statutory definition of Canadian subjects ; and the provisions of the Versailles Treaty concerning the realization of German property and application of the proceeds to the liquidation of debts due from Germans led to the recognition of a class of Australian nationals distinguished from British subjects *simpliciter*.   Again, in 1921 an Act to define Canadian nationals was passed by the Canadian Parliament in order to enable Canada, as a Member of the League of Nations, to nominate candidates for election to membership of the Court (see an article by Professor Berriedale Keith in *The Manchester Guardian*, 4th July, 1927).

[2] Report of the Inter-Imperial Relations Committee, 1926 (*Cmd.* 2768 of 1926), p. 14.   See further Section (ii) below.

'active' belligerency in the case of self-governing communities in the British Empire had been illustrated by the inclusion of clauses— first in the abortive Anglo-French Treaty of Guarantee signed in 1919,[1] then in the Peace Treaty of Lausanne, and then again in the Pact of Locarno, which was signed in 1925 and brought into force in 1926 [2]—which specifically excepted the self-governing Dominions and India from the obligations undertaken in these instruments by Great Britain on behalf of the British Empire, unless and until any of these specified communities in the Empire voluntarily adhered, by their own act, to the instrument in question. The 'Chanāq Incident' of 1922 [3] testified to the same distinction in a sensational way; and even when the danger of a local recrudescence of the General War, which was then in the air, had been removed by the negotiation and signature at Lausanne of a peace treaty between Turkey and those countries (including the British Empire) with which she had not previously ceased to remain at war juridically, the Canadian Prime Minister put it on record that, inasmuch as the Canadian Government had not participated in the negotiation of the Lausanne Treaty, the Canadian ratification of the treaty would only bind Canada 'legally and technically', without imposing on her 'any active obligation beyond that which [the Canadian] Parliament of its own volition' might recognize 'as arising out of the situation'.[4] In the very constitution of the Irish Free State (which was accepted by the Government of Great Britain as being in accord with the Articles of Agreement of 1921) it was similarly provided (Art. 49) that, 'save in the case of actual invasion, the Irish Free State shall not be committed to actual participation in any war without the consent of its Parliament'.

Nevertheless, it remained true—and this not only as a theorem of international law but as an empirical fact of outstanding importance in international affairs—that the British Empire was a single state in relation to foreign countries; and from this apparently plain and simple statement a second paradox emerges. As a single state, the British Empire in 1926 was only one among no less than fifty-eight sovereign independent states then existing in the world.[5]

---

[1] See *Survey for 1920–3*, pp. 58–9.
[2] See *Survey for 1925*, vol. ii, Part I A, Sections (ii) and (iii).
[3] See Section (ii) below.
[4] See Section (v) (*b*) below.
[5] There were at that time fifty-six states members of the League of Nations, of which fifty were sovereign independent states and six were communities in the British Empire with a separate membership from that of the British Empire itself, while there were eight sovereign independent states non-

Yet this single state ' bore no real resemblance ' to its peers inasmuch
as it not only covered from one-sixth to one-fifth of the habitable
surface of the earth and contained from one-fifth to one-fourth of the
living generation of mankind, but included territories in all regions—
climatic and political—of the world, and citizens representing all
the chief living races and civilizations, so that there was no major
problem of human affairs of any description in any part of the world
at that time in which the British Empire was not concerned (and,
incidentally, no possibility of organizing the work of the League of
Nations on regional lines that would not conflict with the British
Empire's world-wide structure).[1] In fact, the British Empire was an
almost complete sample of contemporary human society, so that
many of its internal activities, as well as its external relations, were
truly ' world affairs '.

In illustration of the fact that the British Empire included territories in all climatic regions, it is sufficient to note that, in ' the group
of self-governing communities, composed of Great Britain and the
Dominions ',[2] four states members (Great Britain, the Irish Free
State, Newfoundland,[3] and Canada) were situated in the northern
and the three others (Australia, New Zealand, and South Africa)
in the southern temperate zone, and that the Indian Empire and
almost all the communities of the widely scattered Colonial Empire
lay in the tropical zone which occupied the intervening space. In
North-Western India, and in three Middle Eastern countries— 'Irāq,
Egypt, and the Anglo-Egyptian Sudan—which were intimately
associated with the Empire though not incorporated in it juridically,
the climate had called upon British statesmen and British engineers
to undertake some of the greatest irrigation works recorded in history,
while the farmers of Great Britain and Ireland—' fortunati nimium,
sua si bona norint '—were blessed with an embarrassingly abundant
annual quota of rain.

Among the citizens of this world-wide Empire, the White Race

members of the League (the United States of America, the U.S.S.R., Mexico,
Ecuador, Turkey, Afghanistan, Najd-Hijāz, and the Yaman).

[1] In this connexion see Lord Balfour's criticism of the Draft Treaty of
Mutual Assistance in a speech delivered in the House of Lords on the 24th July,
1924 (passage quoted in the *Survey for 1924*, p. 35).

[2] *Cmd.* 2768 of 1926, p. 14.

[3] For the status of Newfoundland see *op. cit.*, p. 16, footnote. As a self-
governing community in the British Empire she appears to have been on the
same footing as Canada, Australia, South Africa, and New Zealand. On the
other hand, she was not a member of the League of Nations. In 1926 it
seemed probable that other communities in the Empire, e. g. Southern
Rhodesia, would sooner or later reach the position which Newfoundland
occupied at this time.

(or at least its 'Nordic' and 'Mediterranean' varieties) was represented in the European communities of the Empire (which were to be found in the Mediterranean as well as in the British Isles) and in the communities of European origin overseas (which were recruited not only from the European communities of the Empire but from Continental European countries which never had been, and were never likely to be, included in the Empire themselves). The Brown Race was represented in the Indian Empire and Malaya ; the Red Race in Canada ; and the Black Race in a number of African, West Indian, and Melanesian territories, some of which formed part of the Colonial Empire administered by Great Britain, while others were under the administration of self-governing Dominions (either as integral parts of their home territories—the situation in the South African Union, where a White, a Coloured, and a Black population were at that time intermingled—or as Crown Colonies for which a Dominion and not Great Britain was responsible—the status of Papua in relation to the Australian Commonwealth). Even the Yellow Race was represented in the non-self-governing colony of Hongkong and by the Chinese settlers who had become a very important element in certain other portions of the Colonial Empire that lay in the Pacific section of the tropical zone.[1] And the muster was completed by the Maoris and other representatives of the Polynesian Race (so remote geographically from the supposed homelands of the White Race, to which the Polynesian Race nevertheless bore so close a physical resemblance) and by strange survivals of primitive mankind like the Todas of Southern India, the Veddahs of Ceylon, the Blackfellows of Australia, the Bushmen and Hottentots of South Africa, and the Esquimaux in the arctic fringes of the Dominion of Canada.

The five living civilizations, as well as the different races of mankind, were also represented among the citizens of the British Empire. Indeed, the British Indian Empire alone contained within its frontiers almost the whole of contemporary Hindu society except the 500,000 inhabitants of the little island of Bali who were living under Dutch rule. In addition, the Indian Empire contained more than three times as many Muslims (including both Sunnīs and Shī'īs)

---

[1] For these settlers see the *Survey for 1926*, Part III B, Section (vi). The Leased Territory of Weihaiwei is not mentioned in the text, since juridically it had never formed an integral part of the British Empire but had remained under Chinese sovereignty. Moreover, at the Washington Conference of 1921–2 the first step towards the rendition of Weihaiwei to the Chinese Government had been taken by the British Delegation (see *Survey for 1920–3*, pp. 463–4 ; *Survey for 1925*, vol. ii, pp. 377–8).

as the U.S.S.R. and more than six times as many as Turkey (the premier Islamic sovereign independent state in the world) ; yet the Indian Muslim community, though the most considerable, was far from being the only Muslim community in the British Empire, which possessed Muslim citizens and protected persons as far afield as Cyprus and Nigeria and South Africa and Malaya—not to speak of the Muslim populations of Egypt and the Anglo-Egyptian Sudan, of Palestine and 'Irāq, of Maskat and the ' Trucial Chieftainships ' in the Persian Gulf which, though not juridically parts of the Empire, were intimately associated with it in various forms. In point of numbers, Western civilization—the dominant culture of the Empire —was less adequately represented than either Hinduism or Islam. Yet the British communities of Western culture were not unrepresentative of the main divisions of Western Christendom. While Anglicanism, Calvinism, and other varieties of Protestantism were predominant in Great Britain, Northern Ireland, and South Africa, the Irish Free State and the Canadian Province of Quebec were two of the most devoutly Catholic countries in the contemporary world, and in Australia in 1916 almost one-quarter of the Commonwealth electorate was stated (on the authority of the then Prime Minister of the Commonwealth Government, Mr. Hughes) to consist of the Catholic descendants of Irish settlers. As for the two other living civilizations, that of the Far East was represented by the British subjects of Chinese origin and that of Orthodox Christendom by the Greek majority in the population of the Crown Colony of Cyprus. Even the remnants of several extinct civilizations were to be found under the British aegis. India—great mother and foster-mother of civilizations—still harboured, as the prosperous Parsee community, the descendants of those Zoroastrian refugees who in the seventh century after Christ had fled before the face of the first Islamic conquerors of their native Iran. In Burma and Ceylon the Indian and the Colonial Empires comprised two out of the three countries [1] in which Hinayana Buddhism (the dominant culture of India Proper two thousand years earlier) was still alive. In Palestine the British Empire was committed by the Balfour Declaration of 1917, and by a mandate conferred by the Principal Allied Powers and approved by the League of Nations, to the historic task of re-establishing a ' National Home ' for the Jews.[2] In exercising its trusteeship for 'Irāq, the British Empire had secured frontiers for this new state which—so long as the sovereign independence of 'Irāq continued

---

[1] The third surviving Hinayana Buddhist country was the sovereign independent state of Siam.   [2] See *H. P. C.*, vol. vi, pp. 170–7.

to be governed by the existing Anglo-'Irāqī treaty [1]—would assure
the protection of the Assyrian Christians in the Zagros highlands
(all that survived from the flock of a Nestorian Patriarch of Seleucia
whose Patriarchate had once stretched from the Euphrates to Sianfu
and from the Altai Mountains to Cape Comorin) [2] and of the mysterious Yazīdīs of Ba'idhrah and the Jabal Sinjar, who naïvely took
advantage of the supposed benevolence of Almighty God by directing
their propitiatory efforts towards Satan in the image of a brazen
peacock.

Besides all this, the British Empire had given hostages to Fortune
in every one of those great political regions of the contemporary
world which were the several theatres of international affairs—that
is, in so far as the movement of international affairs had not yet fully
become (as it was rapidly becoming) an indivisible drama enacted
on one world-wide stage. The recent invention of aircraft had already
begun to bind the island of Great Britain—which was described in
1924, by a great British Foreign Minister in a felicitous phrase, as
'the nerve-centre' of the British Empire [3]—to the Continent of Europe
'by ties as light as air and as strong as links of iron' (an unexpected
application, in a startling literal sense, of a famous figure of speech
which another British statesman had struck out, a hundred and fifty
years before, in order to express an ideal of political association
afterwards achieved in the relations between Great Britain and the
self-governing communities of the British Empire overseas).[4]

In old days—Britain being an island which, as long as its sea power
[was] retained, could not be attacked on its own soil—Europe might
be convulsed but the British nerve-centre, lying in the Ocean outside
Europe, would be protected by this position and would not only preserve
its own vitality but also its communications with other parts of the
Empire, while Europe was convulsed on land ; but to-day things have
changed. Britain, the nerve-centre, is no longer in the old sense an
island. In old days Continental armies could not come to Britain as
long as the British fleet dominated the seas. That cannot be said now.

[1] See *Survey for 1925*, vol. i, Part III, Section (x).
[2] The Indian Christians in Travancore and adjoining parts of the Indian
Empire had also formerly belonged to the Nestorian Church ; but in the
seventeenth century after Christ they had transferred their allegiance to an
itinerant Syrian Monophysite Patriarch of Antioch, in the mistaken belief
that he was their long-lost shepherd.
[3] Address by Lord Grey on ' The Dominions and Foreign Policy ', broad-
casted on the 14th November, 1924, under the auspices of the British Institute
of International Affairs (*The Times*, 15th November, 1924).
[4] ' My hold of the Colonies is in the close affection which grows from common
names, from kindred blood, from similar privileges and equal protection.
These are ties which, though light as air, are as strong as links of iron '—
Edmund Burke, *Speech on Conciliation with America*, 1775.

The Channel could not be kept open for British shipping if there were big guns on the south shore of it in hostile hands. Aircraft can cross the Channel for hostile purposes with less difficulty than armies can cross rivers. The risk of Britain being involved in Continental complications is greater than it ever was.[1]

√ While Great Britain was thus gradually being welded, by the irresistible progress of Western scientific invention, on to the most dangerous of the continents, the Pacific—on which three out of the six fully-governing communities in the Empire possessed seaboards —was threatening to belie its name by becoming the most dangerous of the oceans ; and the continent of Africa, until recently a dark and unknown void which served to insulate South Africa (now another self-governing community in the Empire) from the rest of the world, had suddenly been opened up by Western enterprise, with a revolutionary effect of which it was as yet impossible to foresee the outcome.

Even more revolutionary was the fermentation which had set in, since the General War of 1914–18, in the Islamic World—a region which intervened between Europe and Russia on the one side and Tropical Africa, India, the Far East, and the Pacific on the other,[2] and which thus commanded one of the three main lines of communication between different parts of the British Empire.[3] On the Mediterranean sea-route from the British Isles to India, Australia, New Zealand, Malaya, and Hongkong, the Moroccan coast commanded the Straits of Gibraltar as effectively as the French and Belgian coasts commanded the Straits of Dover ; the Suez Canal traversed Egyptian territory ; Aden was an enclave in the Islamic sub-continent of Arabia ; and a portion of the Aden Protectorate was at this time actually under the military occupation of the Imām of San'ā, the sovereign of the independent Islamic state of the Yaman. Singapore itself—an emporium of Imperial trade and a prospective Imperial naval base which commanded the Straits of Malacca, where the easternmost section of this great Imperial sea-route began—was encircled by an archipelago which (including Netherlands India and the Philippines, as well as British Malaya) contained a Muslim population not less than fifty million strong.

The least dangerous of the political regions which held hostages

[1] Lord Grey, in the address cited above. Compare a similar passage (quoted in the *Survey for 1924*, footnote to pp. 27–8) in a speech delivered by Lord Grey in the House of Lords on the 24th July, 1924, on the occasion of a debate on the limitation of armaments.

[2] See *Survey for 1925*, vol. i, Introduction.

[3] These three lines of communication were the trans-Atlantic sea-route to Canada and the two alternative sea-routes to India and Australasia, one round the Cape of Good Hope and the other through the Mediterranean.

of the British Empire at this time was the continent of America. Yet Canada, the senior self-governing Dominion of the British Crown overseas, stood possessed (as has been mentioned above) of the perilous asset of a Pacific seaboard ; and the Caribbean Sea, whose coasts and islands were studded with British Crown Colonies which had been happy in having had no history for the best part of a century, was being drawn again—by the cutting of the Panama Canal and the southward trend of United States ' imperialism '— into the vortex of international affairs. Indeed, it was significant of the ' dangerous living ' to which the British Empire was committed at this time that the least dangerous political region, from the British point of view, should be the continent on which the United States had become the paramount Power. It was true that the expansion of the United States no longer threatened the security of any American community in the British Empire, as it continued to threaten the security of some, at least, of the Latin-American Republics. The unfortified frontier between the United States and Canada—stretching as it did from Atlantic to Pacific over a length of 3,898 miles—was the greatest triumph of voluntary reciprocal disarmament on the part of two states with a common land frontier and without a common sovereignty that had yet been achieved in the modern world ; and, at the fifth session of the Assembly of the League of Nations at Geneva in the autumn of 1924, the Canadian delegate, in the speech in which he announced his intention to submit the draft Protocol to his Government, was fully justified in reminding his colleagues that his countrymen ' lived in a fire-proof house ', protected by the whole breadth of the Atlantic from the danger of a European conflagration. Indeed Canada, who, so far from having anything now to fear from her only neighbour on land, could count on the American as well as the British fleet to guard her against overseas invasion, was at this time probably the best secured country in the world. Yet this fact, while altogether advantageous for Canada herself and therefore not disadvantageous for the British Empire, in which the good of the whole was inseparable from the good of the constituent communities, was nevertheless a possible source of embarrassment for the Empire in its foreign relations. Before the War of 1914–18 Great Britain and Canada had both, in different degrees, enjoyed the advantages of insularity. Since the War their respective situations, in the matter of security, had become sharply differentiated. While Great Britain seemed to be in danger of forfeiting her insular security through being welded, by links of air, on to the European continent, Canada, who shared with

the United States, on an amicable footing, the ownership and occupation of the vast island of North America, had seen her security
notably increased, since the War, by the rise of the United States
to the highest degree of potency among the surviving Great Powers ;
and for this reason Canadian opinion could not fail to be influenced
by the determined effort which this American Great Power had been
making, from 1919 onwards, to disengage herself from political commitments on the farther side of the Atlantic. The influence of
United States policy was not indeed strong enough to deter Canada
from entering the League of Nations—a step which recommended
itself to Canada partly on account of her ties with Great Britain (who
evidently could not have adopted the American policy, even if
Canada had done so) and partly because admission to separate
membership in the League, in their own rights, constituted, for
Canada and the other self-governing Dominions of the British
Empire overseas, an international registration of a status which was
already recognized by Great Britain as theirs but which had not
previously received any formal recognition that would be valid in
international law.   Nevertheless, though Canada did not refrain
from entering the League, it was noteworthy that she worked
actively and persistently for a modification of Article 10 of the
League Covenant [1]—the clause which had been one of the chief
specific stumbling-blocks in the path of the Senate of the United
States when they kept the United States out of the League by their
non-ratification of the Treaty of Versailles.

From the foregoing survey it will be seen that the British Empire
was not only concerned in all the world-wide problems of international affairs at this time, but that different communities in the
Empire were concerned in these problems in different degrees and
in different ways.

The British Empire as a whole—having given hostages to Fortune
in every part of the world—had a greater stake in the problem of
security than any other state ; for, although the hostages of the
Empire in each several region might be less insecure than other
states in that region (as, for instance, in Europe Great Britain was
evidently less insecure than Poland and on the American Continent
Canada less than Mexico), it was clear that the moderate but world-
wide dangers to which the Empire was exposed amounted to a
greater sum, in the aggregate, than the acute danger to which a
' state with limited interests ' like Poland or like Mexico was exposed
in some single region. It was also clear that, for the British Empire,

---

[1] See Section (iii) (c) below.

the danger was enhanced by the special complexity of the problem as it presented itself to the various communities of this world-wide ' political organization '. For the Empire as a whole the greatest danger, in the period following the General War of 1914–18, was the possibility of a serious conflict with the United States over the interpretation of maritime law. For the ' nerve-centre ' of the Empire, Great Britain, security was first and foremost a European problem in which she had to reckon with France and Germany, and in the second place a Mediterranean problem in which she had to reckon with France, Italy, and the Islamic World. For Canada, it was first and foremost an American problem in which she had to reckon with the United States and indeed depended for her very existence upon the maintenance of peace and goodwill between that American Power and Great Britain, and in the second place a Pacific problem in which she had to reckon with Japan and could count on the support of the United States, Australia, and New Zealand. For the two South Sea Dominions, again, security was wholly a Pacific question in which the United States and Canada had a more direct concern than had Great Britain, so that, in the last resort, the maintenance of trans-Pacific sea-communications with North America might be more important for Australia and New Zealand than the maintenance of sea-communications with the British Isles across the Indian Ocean and the Mediterranean— notwithstanding the fact that, in the first instance, they would naturally look for support to the British and not to the United States Navy.

Again, the Empire as a whole was deeply interested in the many-sided world-problem of migration,[1] and here also from several different and even opposing points of view. For example, two self-governing communities of the Empire—Great Britain and the Irish Free State—were, next to Italy, the chief Western ' countries of emigration ' at that time ; and India was one of the three chief Oriental ' countries of emigration ' (the other two being China and Japan). On the other hand, three of the self-governing Dominions of the Empire overseas—Canada, Australia, and New Zealand— together with more than one of the lesser self-governing communities overseas, such as Southern Rhodesia, were numbered among the ' countries of immigration ', alongside of the United States, Argentina, Uruguay, Brazil, and France. Moreover, the sharp difference of interest and attitude which had declared itself, between these two

---

[1] For an American view of this matter, see an article by John Carter in *The New York Times*, 4th April, 1926.

groups of countries, since the termination of the General War,[1] was by no means less acute as between the respective representatives of the two groups within the British Empire than as between sovereign independent states such as the United States and Italy or the United States and Japan. For Great Britain, oppressed since the War by the burden and menace of unemployment among her industrial population on an unprecedented scale, the incentive to find outlets for emigration was particularly strong. On the other hand, the interest of Canada, Australia, and New Zealand was to direct and control the inflow of immigrants in such a manner as not to flood their markets with immigrant labour of a type or a quantity which it was beyond their capacity to absorb. Their main problem was to preserve a due balance between the agricultural population in their countrysides (which must be the centre of gravity of their economic life for many years to come, however great might be their industrial ambitions for the future) and the industrial population in their cities (where the inflow of urban immigrants threatened to aggravate the drain of population from country to town which at this time was no less pronounced in the young countries of European origin overseas than in the old countries of Europe). Thus, for the Canadian (or Australian or New Zealand) immigration authorities, an industrial worker from Wigan or Glasgow might be a less desirable candidate for an immigration permit than a peasant from Finland or Würtemberg or Hungary ; [2] and the Canadian Government had not only the right but the duty, as the responsible Government of a self-governing community, to take in this matter whatever action was in the national interest of Canada. Subject to this paramount right and duty, the Canadian Government could and did take concerted action with the Government of Great Britain for the special assistance of immigration into Canada from that country ; but Canada could not be, and was not, expected by Great Britain deliberately to transfer any part of the problem of unemployment on to her own shoulders.

In the matter of Oriental migration, again, there was a conflict of

[1] For the difference of policy between ' countries of emigration ' and ' countries of immigration ' see *Survey for 1924*, Part I B, Section (v).

[2] In recognition of this truth, it had actually been suggested that the best and most economical means of developing Australia as a field for British immigration might be to encourage Scandinavian peasants and farmers to settle in the country, on the calculation that these would make the best immediate rural settlers and that the rural development which they would produce would stimulate urban development and so indirectly but effectively increase the openings in Australia for industrial and other urban immigrants from Great Britain.

interest between India on the one hand and the overseas Dominions of European origin on the other ; and this gave rise to greater searchings of heart than the maladjustment of interests between the same Dominions and Great Britain because, in the case of Oriental migration, the economic issue was complicated by a marked difference in the standard of living and this difference itself was the outward symptom of racial and cultural differences which were capable of arousing the strongest of all social passions. Indeed, at that time the controversy over the status of British subjects of Indian race who were lawfully domiciled in the self-governing Dominion of South Africa and in the Crown Colony of Kenya was creating such tension that, if South Africa and India had been sovereign independent states, they would almost certainly have broken off diplomatic relations. As it was, they were fortunately debarred from venting their feelings in this way, since (another paradox) there was an absence in inter-Imperial relations, even between self-governing communities, of those regular diplomatic channels of communication that were of old standing in relations between independent states. Accordingly, the South African and the Indian Governments were reduced, by the logical method of exhaustion and by the good offices of other states members of the British Commonwealth, to settling their controversy by friendly consultation.

Finally, the British Empire was intimately concerned in the problem of the contact of civilizations—one of the most important world-problems of the age—which at that time was arising in large measure out of contacts between different sections of that quarter of the living generation of mankind who happened to be ' British subjects '. In the Indian Empire Hinduism and Islam were in collision with Western civilization and simultaneously in more violent collision with one another. In East and South Africa another ' three-cornered ' conflict was arising between native Africans and Indian and Western immigrants. In the Pacific there was an antagonism between Far Eastern and Western civilization which imported an additional danger into those problems of migration and security in which the three self-governing communities of the Empire with Pacific seaboards were involved.

Such, in broad outline, were the great problems of Imperial foreign policy and inter-Imperial relations. In the Report of the Inter-Imperial Relations Committee which was adopted on the 19th November, 1926, by the Imperial Conference then sitting in London, ' it was frankly recognized ' that in the conduct of foreign affairs generally, ' as in the sphere of defence, the major share of

1926

responsibility' rested at that time, 'and must for some time continue to rest, with His Majesty's Government in Great Britain ' ; [1] and this Government, being the Government of a self-governing nation, met that responsibility by drawing upon the political experience which the British people in Great Britain had accumulated.[2] In such circumstances a politically inexperienced people—finding itself responsible, through its Government, for the welfare of an Empire which consisted of communities scattered throughout the world, concerned in all the dangerous world-problems, and approaching each of these problems from different and often conflicting stand-points—might have taken refuge in logic and insisted that it could not shoulder a major share of so heavy a responsibility without retaining in its own hands a paramount control over the conduct of the whole common weal. So far from this, the British people dealt with the situation by devolving upon as many as possible of the other communities in the Empire, at the fastest possible rate, the greatest possible measure of self-government with all its implications.

To avoid misapprehension, it may be well to recall, in passing, that in 1926 the communities towards which this policy was applied were none of them styled sovereign independent states. There were indeed a number of titularly sovereign independent states which

---

[1] *Cmd.* 2768 of 1926, pp. 25–6.

[2] Attention was drawn to this difference in the amount of political experience at the disposal of British statesmanship, in Great Britain and in the Dominions respectively, in a series of articles published in *The Times* on the 2nd, 3rd, 4th, 5th, and 6th February, 1925 :

Great Britain is in a special position for another reason. Her political traditions enshrine the experience of international dealing of many centuries. She possesses an excellent and world-wide diplomatic service, and her people contain an extraordinary percentage of ex-Ambassadors, Governors, High Commissioners and other public officials, who have had first-hand experience in all parts of the globe, and who spend their time in educating the public opinion of their country about the outside world, in Parliament, through the Press, from the platform. Great Britain has external interests, and a nervous system which probably keeps her in closer touch with world affairs than any other country on the earth.

The position of the Dominions is entirely different. Until the World War they had none of them had any direct experience of an international kind. They were young communities, almost entirely absorbed in the arduous work of settling empty territory, building houses, roads, railways, schools, and the other primary equipment of national, political, and economic life. Not one of them had any diplomatic service or any means apart from occasional newspaper articles of first-hand information about world affairs.

The same point was made by the Prime Minister of Australia, Mr. Bruce, in a speech delivered to the Pilgrims' Association of the United States at New York on the 29th December, 1926 (Text in *International Conciliation,* No. 228; see pp. 138–9).

were intimately associated with the British Empire. Apart from the two states of 'Irāq and Palestine, there were Egypt (a country of great wealth and great geographical importance, with 15,000,000 inhabitants) and such lesser luminaries as the Sultanate of Maskat and the ' Trucial Chieftainships ' in the Persian Gulf. Yet in this matter of independence the British Empire indulged its paradoxical genius to the last degree. The titular sovereignty and independence of the states aforementioned was hedged about with so many reservations and conditions on the part of His Britannic Majesty's Governments in Great Britain [1] and in India that their juridical status had to be regarded as a relic of the past or an earnest of the future rather than a full present reality.[2] On the other hand, those communities within the Empire which His Majesty's Government in Great Britain had invested with ' Dominion Status ' in satisfaction of their desires and in accordance with the will of the people of Great Britain enjoyed a plenitude of self-government not to be found elsewhere except in sovereign and independent states, though in juridical form these communities remained integral parts of an empire which was still a unitary state in international law.

A British historian who attempts to treat of ' Dominion Status ' must be on his guard against the common human weakness of over-estimating one's own achievements—a danger which is notoriously even more insidious when the achievement is that of some great society or community, of which the individual is an insignificant member, than in matters of personal concern. Nevertheless, the conjecture may be hazarded that the emergence of ' Dominion Status ' was one example of a contemporary development which, in biological language, might be termed a new ' variation ' or even

[1] In the case of Palestine, the reservations and conditions provisionally restricting Palestinian independence were contained in the mandate conferred upon Great Britain by the Principal Allied and Associated Powers and approved by the League of Nations.

[2] While this book was in the press, the number of the reservations was increased by the following passage in a note addressed on the 19th May, 1928, by the British Secretary of State for Foreign Affairs, Sir Austen Chamberlain, to the U.S. Secretary of State, Mr. Kellogg, in the course of a diplomatic correspondence regarding the conclusion of a pact for the renunciation of war as an instrument of national policy :

'. . . There are certain regions of the world the welfare and integrity of which constitute a special and vital interest for our peace and safety. His Majesty's Government have been at pains to make it clear in the past that interference with these regions cannot be suffered. Their protection against attack is to the British Empire a measure of self-defence. It must be clearly understood that His Majesty's Government in Great Britain accept the new treaty upon the distinct understanding that it does not prejudice their freedom of action in this respect ' (*Cmd.* 3109 of 1928, p. 25).

' mutation ' in the political life of mankind.   At any rate, the
emergence of ' Dominion Status ' had been accompanied by the
evolution, within the chrysalis of the British Empire, of a wholly
new creature, the British Commonwealth of Self-Governing Nations ;
and no doubt this creative achievement was the special mark of the
British Empire which was held to justify the bold assertion (cited at
the beginning of this introduction) that in 1926 that Empire bore
no real resemblance to any other political organization which then
existed or had ever yet been tried.

In 1926, in the judgement of the Inter-Imperial Relations Committee of the Imperial Conference of that year, ' the group of self-
governing communities composed of Great Britain and the Dominions '
had, ' as regards all vital matters, reached its full development ' ; [1]
and the Committee went on to declare that ' their position and
mutual relation ' might ' be readily defined ': 'They are autonomous
Communities within the British Empire, equal in status, in no way
subordinate one to another in any aspect of their domestic or external
affairs, though united by a common allegiance to the Crown, and
freely associated as members of the British Commonwealth of
Nations.' [2]

The authors of this definition added that ' every self-governing
member of the Empire ' was ' now master of its own destiny ', and
that ' in fact, if not always in form, it ' was ' subject to no compulsion
whatever '.   And this was merely an abbreviation of a definition
which had been given in March 1920 by another distinguished
British statesman (himself of Canadian birth), Mr. Bonar Law :

> What is the essential of Dominion Home Rule ?   The essential is that
> they have control of their whole destinies, of their fighting forces, and
> of the amounts which they will contribute to the general security of
> the Empire.   All these things are vital, and there is not a man in the
> House who would not admit that the connexion of the Dominions with
> the Empire depends upon themselves.   If the self-governing Dominions
> of Australia or Canada choose to-morrow to say ' We will no longer make
> a part of the British Empire ' we would not try to force them.   Dominion
> Home Rule means the right to decide for themselves.[3]

[1] To a detached onlooker this might seem a bold assertion for the statesmen of the Commonwealth to venture upon at a time when so many elements
in the organic structure of the Commonwealth appeared to be growing and
changing so vigorously.
[2] Cmd. 2768 of 1926, p. 14.
[3] This was strictly true, but it was not quite the whole truth ; for the fact
that the Dominions were no longer held within the British Empire by any
sanction imposed by Great Britain did not mean that they were subject to
no sanction at all.   The real sanction which practically precluded secession
at this time, and would probably continue to preclude it for a long time to

One decision which the Dominions had made during the Peace Conference of Paris—and this with the full concurrence and support of Great Britain—was to claim and secure admission to separate membership, in their own rights, in the League of Nations ; and this claim had not been rejected by the other sovereign states with which the British Empire was co-operating in the foundation of the League, since the parts which the Dominions had played in the General War constituted titles to nationhood which could hardly be invalidated by such a technicality as the lack of titular sovereign independence. Thus the names of Canada, Australia, New Zealand, South Africa, and India appeared (slightly ' set forward ' by a diplomatically instructed printer) in the list of original Members of the League of Nations in the text of the Treaty of Versailles ; and the establishment of the Irish Free State in 1922 was followed in due course by the admission to the League of this new self-governing state member of the British Commonwealth in 1923. In this matter, too, there are several paradoxes to be recorded.

First, Great Britain, alone among the self-governing states members of the British Commonwealth, did not ask for or receive separate representation in the League, any more than she had required separate representation at the Peace Conference of Paris. At Paris the British Empire, as a Unitary Great Power, had been represented (under a domestic arrangement agreed upon by the British Imperial War Cabinet) by a delegation on which representatives of India and the Dominions took their turns in sitting side by side with the representatives of the then United Kingdom ; and in addition the Dominions, with the support of the British Empire delegation, had induced the other parties to the Conference to agree to their also being represented separately on the same terms as the lesser Allied states.[1] Thus the British Dominions, not content with being the only communities without titular sovereignty and independence that were represented at the Conference, secured representation twice over in two different capacities—' a peculiarly effective position ' (as Sir Robert Borden described it in retrospect) which was not enjoyed by any Great Power. On the other hand, Great Britain was content,

come, was the certainty that no Government, party, or national element in any Dominion could propose secession without splitting the country to such an extent as to imperil the national unity of that Dominion itself. In other words, the sanction to which each Dominion was subject was internal and not external ; but possibly it was all the stronger for that.

[1] See the account given by Sir Robert Borden to the Canadian House of Commons on the 2nd September, 1919, as quoted in *The Round Table*, September 1924.

at the Conference, not to have any separate representation at all; and the method of representation at the Conference seems to have suggested the formula of membership in the League, in which the British Empire, the self-governing Dominions, and India, but not Great Britain, separately appeared.[1]

Another paradox was that whereas, in Article 1 of the League Covenant, it was laid down that no state should be admitted subsequently to the League that was not 'fully self-governing', the list of original Members included India—a dependency of the British Empire which on the 10th January, 1920 (the date on which the Versailles Treaty, containing the League Covenant, came into force), had only just started upon that course of evolution towards Dominion Status which was inaugurated by the coming into force on the 23rd December, 1919, of the Government of India Act.

In the light of these facts, it may certainly be stated that the representation of the British Empire in the League of Nations bore ' no real resemblance ' to that of any other Member or Members. Yet it was possible to press the doctrine of the uniqueness of the British Empire too far. Granting that the Commonwealth of Nations was a new ' variation ' or ' mutation ' in political structure, it was a well-observed feature of evolution in general that such new departures usually declared themselves, not in some unique sport of Nature, but in several contemporary incarnations. In asserting that the British Empire bore ' no real resemblance to any other political organization which ' then existed or had ' ever yet been tried ', the Inter-Imperial Relations Committee of 1926 were possibly overlooking certain resemblances of structure, procedure, and aim between the British Commonwealth of Nations (the element in the Empire to which their dictum presumably referred),[2] and that international League of Nations of which all the states members of the Commonwealth were states members likewise.

These resemblances may be set out under the following heads :

(i) *Full self-government was a necessary qualification for membership* in both organizations (with the same anomalous temporary exception, in both, in favour of India). In the League the application of

---

[1] In practice, the representation of the British Empire in the League was not put into commission between His Majesty's Governments in Great Britain and in the self-governing Dominions and in India, as it had been in the Peace Conference, but was reserved for His Majesty's Government in Great Britain acting not only for Great Britain but for the non-self-governing Colonial Empire.

[2] The non-self-governing Colonial Empire was not, of course, a unique phenomenon. It bore a ' real resemblance ' to the contemporary French, Dutch, and Belgian Colonial Empires, as well as to a number of extinct empires of the kind.

this rule may be studied by examining the procedure followed at the admission of new members (e.g. the Irish Free State in 1923, Abyssinia in 1923, Germany in 1926). In the Commonwealth a recognition of the same principle was implicit in the participation of the Prime Minister of the small self-governing island of Newfoundland in the Imperial Conferences of 1923 and 1926, as well as in the treatment, at the Imperial Conference of 1926, of the colony of Southern Rhodesia, which had attained to self-government in 1925. In his statement at the first sitting of the Conference on the 19th October, 1926, Mr. Amery, the British Secretary of State for Dominion Affairs, announced that, inasmuch as Southern Rhodesia was now a self-governing part of the Empire, and, though not a Dominion and as such separately represented at the Imperial Conference, was undoubtedly interested in some of the subjects on the agenda, more particularly on the economic side, he was proposing— after consultation with the Premier of Southern Rhodesia, and if the proposal met with the approval of the Conference—to ask the High Commissioner for Southern Rhodesia to assist him in matters where Southern Rhodesia's interests were concerned.

(ii) *The powers and functions of a super-state were as studiously disclaimed by both organizations as they were jealously denied to them by their respective states members.* In reference to the League, this proposition may be illustrated by the jealousy of certain states members (e.g. Australia) which happened to be 'countries of immigration' lest the League might impinge upon the prescriptive right of self-governing states to control immigration into their own territories, at their absolute discretion, by their municipal laws (a jealousy which declared itself during the discussions on the Protocol for the Pacific Settlement of International Disputes which had been drafted at the fifth session of the League Assembly in 1924).[1] It may be illustrated, again, by the objections offered to the questionnaire which the Permanent Mandates Commission circulated to Mandatory Powers in 1926.[2] Such jealousies were less unreasonable in the Commonwealth, where it was not a question of imposing a hypothetical super-state upon states members which stood possessed of an acknowledged sovereignty and independence, but of evolving the new political 'variation' of Dominion Status out of a unitary British Empire, which had actually been a super-state *de jure* and *de facto* in regard to the Dominions themselves in the past, and was still such in respect of the non-self-governing communities that constituted the Colonial

[1] See *Survey for 1924*, pp. 55–9, and *Survey for 1925*, vol. ii, pp. 2–3.
[2] This matter will be dealt with in a subsequent volume.

Empire of the British Crown. The anxiety to secure some explicit and formal recognition of the fact that the British Empire had ceased altogether to be a super-state as far as the Dominions were concerned was naturally most evident in those Dominions whose relations with the Empire in the recent past had been least happy. In Ireland this anxiety was manifested during the negotiation of the Articles of Agreement of 1921, was recorded in the texts of the Agreement itself and of the Constitution of the Free State, and was expressed during the next few years in the policy of the Free State in such matters as the candidature of the Free State in 1926 for a temporary seat on the Council of the League of Nations [1] and the exercise in 1924 of the right to accredit a separate diplomatic representative to the President of the United States [2]—a right which accrued to the Irish Free State, on the most-favoured-Dominion-treatment principle which had been embodied in the Articles, in virtue of an agreement made in 1920 between the Governments of Great Britain and Canada,[3] of which the Free State took advantage before Canada herself. In South Africa a similar anxiety was originally present, and afterwards allayed, in the mind of General Hertzog (the leader of the Afrikander-Nationalist Party, which had been founded on a programme of secession from the Empire), whose change of attitude in consequence of his experience at the Imperial Conference of 1926 was thrown into relief owing to the frankness with which the General was accustomed to declare his sentiments in their successive phases. On the 22nd April, 1926, in the course of a passage of arms in the South African Parliament between General Hertzog and General Smuts on the question whether the international status of the Union was to be put to the test by the South African Prime Minister at the forthcoming Imperial Conference, General Hertzog accused General Smuts of maintaining that ' there must be in the Empire some super-power, or otherwise disintegration would result '—an accusation which General Smuts repudiated.[4]

I regard the British Empire [General Smuts took occasion to declare] as an organic combination of equal states, and the Prime Minister will find that that is the attitude of every Dominion Prime Minister and British Prime Minister. There is no super-state, no super-authority. It is a meeting of equals under one sovereign.[5]

[1] See Section (iii) (d) below.   [2] See Section (iv) (c) below.
[3] See Section (iv) (b) below.
[4] The Times, 23rd April, 1926. For an exposition of General Hertzog's attitude at this time, see the speech which he delivered at Stellenbosch on the 15th May, 1926 (Ibid., 18th May, 1926).
[5] Ibid., 23rd April, 1926.

In his opening speech, at the first sitting of the Imperial Conference on the 19th October, 1926,[1] General Hertzog—after stating the (uncontested) proposition ' that the corner-stone of the Empire is the will, the goodwill of those who compose it ', and that ' without that will the Empire must collapse '—did raise the question ' whether at present all the conditions ' were ' there to ensure the permanency of that will, and therefore of the Empire ' ; and, ' speaking merely for South Africa', he expressed the opinion that they were not present.

South Africa is anxious to possess that will equally with every other member of the Commonwealth, but that will can be assured for the future only if she can be made to feel implicit faith in her full and free nationhood upon the basis of equality with every other member of the Commonwealth. That implicit faith she does not possess to-day, but she will possess it the moment her independent national status has ceased to be a matter in dispute and has become internationally recognized.

The question thus raised by the South African Prime Minister received its answer in the Report (many times quoted above) of the Inter-Imperial Relations Committee of which General Hertzog himself was a member (a report which was adopted unanimously by the Imperial Conference exactly one month later) ; and in the speeches which he delivered in South Africa upon his return home General Hertzog bore public testimony to his political conversion.[2] At Capetown on the 13th December, 1926 :

He said emphatically that he no longer feared the Empire. He confessed that he had been a lifelong opponent of Imperialism and had feared the Empire. That was because the Empire had been represented as a sort of super-State, but this conception had been scotched by the Imperial Conference. There was no question any longer of domination or superiority over the Dominions. Each was now free to follow its own will. That made all the difference to his thoughts of the Empire, which would never be conceived of in future as a super-State over the Dominions. He added a remarkable declaration about the English-speaking South Africans. He said they naturally felt love and reverence for the country of their descent. He could not feel that ; it would be absurd of him to pretend to ; but if he were a South African of English descent, he would feel all the more love and respect for Great Britain as the country which, through free institutions and a common-sense use of them, had brought the younger nations to being ' as free as the Motherland and at the same time standing in the closest tie of affection '.

[1] Text in *Cmd.* 2769 of 1927, pp. 23–5.
[2] The conversion of the Transvaal Nationalists, who were at first sceptical (*The Times*, 25th November, 1926), was formally announced, before General Hertzog's return from London, by the Chairman of the Party, Mr. Tielman Roos (who was also Acting Prime Minister and Minister of Justice), in a speech delivered at Springs, as reported in *The Times* of the 3rd December, 1926.

He added that South Africans, of whatever descent, were and would remain South Africans first, exercising their power of freedom in the interests of their own country. They could leave the question of separation from the British group to a problematic future.[1]

Again, at Paarl on the 14th, he declared that it was hardly believable that the struggle for full, unbounded liberty for South Africa as a people was over; yet it was so, and they must simply accept this for the future.

Referring to the report on Inter-Imperial Relations adopted by the Imperial Conference, he said no declaration could be devised by which the country's liberty in a most unlimited manner could be so clearly demonstrated as was done in the document as it stood. No one need bother in future about South Africa breaking away from the Empire. As a result of the work of the Imperial Conference, the old Empire no longer existed. The old Empire was a dominating State under which South Africa and the other Dominions had to, and did, submit for years. All that remained was a free alliance of England and the six Dominions, co-operating as friends and, so to speak, forming their own League of Nations. The will binding them thereto was their own will, and if to-morrow they wanted to get out they would go out. When they spoke of the Empire to-day it meant the name given to seven Free States, all freely co-operating in so far as they wanted to do so and as long as they wanted to do so. The Englishman need not fear that they would say farewell to the Empire, because it was in their interests not to do so. He felt that if the old Empire had been persisted with there would have been a probability of its going to pieces.[2]

Finally, at Pretoria on the 20th:

He said that South Africa was now free in its self-government, inside as well as outside, and the degree and the nature of that self-government were equal to those of Great Britain, without any inferiority or reservation. It could make no difference whether one spoke of autonomy, independence, or sovereign independence. It was sufficient for them to know that their status and liberty were no less than those of Great Britain, and they did not object that this could, as a matter of fact, not be greater than that of the most powerful free nation in Europe. Any kind of idea of supreme authority inside the Empire had been finally dispelled by the Imperial Conference. Neither Great Britain nor any Dominion recognized any authority over itself except its own national free will. The result of the Imperial Conference was the positive, complete equalization of national liberty and rights without any reservation, openly declared and accepted by qualified representatives of the Governments of Great Britain and the Dominions. Now that the Union had been openly acknowledged as an independent free State, he personally did not hesitate to declare that the welfare and happiness of South Africa could along no other course be better maintained and fostered than within the union of nations with which she was now associated as a free people of her own free will, and that in no other

[1] *The Times*, 14th December, 1926.   [2] *Ibid.*, 15th December, 1926.

manner could her national freedom enjoy greater authority and guarantee than within the British Empire on the basis which existed to-day.[1]

(iii) *The settlement of questions of common interest by unanimous decisions reached through consultation*, in contrast to the method of decision by a majority vote, was characteristic of both the League and the Commonwealth—being, in fact, virtually the sole possible method of co-operation between fully self-governing states. In the written constitution of the League the prevalence of ' the unanimity rule ' was one of the conspicuous features ; in the unwritten constitution of the Commonwealth it was one of the fundamental constitutional conventions.[2] ' If I may state in a few words the principle which should guide us in matters of general Imperial interest,' General Hertzog declared at the Imperial Conference of 1926 in his opening speech on the 19th October, ' I would say : in principle, unrestrained freedom of action to each individual member of the Commonwealth ; in practice, consultation with a view to co-operative action wherever possible.' [3]

(iv) *The ' outlawry of war '*, which, as between sovereign independent states, was one of the cardinal aims of the League—imperfectly secured in the Covenant, sought and ensued with perhaps too logical an exactitude in the draft Geneva Protocol of 1924, and not yet completed in 1926—was part of the birthright inherited from the British Empire by the states members of the British Commonwealth, who had attained to full self-government in their relations with the Empire and with one another without acquiring—or dreaming of taking to themselves—the sinister right of going to war with one another.

(v) *The distinction between ' passive ' and ' active ' belligerency* in wars in which the whole ' political organization ' was concerned had arisen in the practice of both the League and the Commonwealth, though it was still a most heretical and indeed a preposterous [4]

[1] *The Times*, 21st December, 1926.
[2] See Sir Robert Borden's remarks on the observance of this convention in the British Empire Delegation at the Peace Conference of Paris, in *The Yale Review*, July 1923.   [3] *Cmd.* 2769 of 1927, p. 24.
[4] Preposterous because illogical, since no modification of the relation between ' enemies ' would arise from it : i. e. the decision of one belligerent to remain ' passive ' would not deprive the enemy of his freedom to exercise his belligerency in the active form. Nor, for that matter, would it exempt the belligerent who had decided to remain ' passive ' from the obligation of taking a number of very serious positive steps. He would still have to close his harbours to enemy ships and intern any enemy ships that happened to be lying in them ; intern enemy subjects that happened to be resident in his territory ; prohibit his own people from trading with the enemy ; and interfere drastically with the freedom of action of neutrals.

doctrine in the eyes of international law as guided by the international practice of the past. Under the Covenant of the League,
Article 16, all states members were pledged to break off economic
relations with any state, member or non-member, which might resort
to war in disregard of its covenants under Articles 12, 13, or 15 ; but,
although a ' covenant-breaking ' state was to be deemed *ipso facto*
to have committed an act of war, the manner and degree of active
co-operation in the task of bringing a ' covenant-breaking ' state to
reason in any particular case was left to the discretion of each state
member of the League in its capacity as a self-governing community.
In the unwritten constitution of the British Commonwealth, in the
event of the British Empire finding itself at war, there had been
established precisely the same distinction between the ' passive '
belligerency to which all communities in the Empire stood committed
automatically and the ' active ' belligerency in respect of which the
self-governing communities of the Commonwealth each possessed
full and exclusive discretion as far as concerned themselves.[1]

These undoubted resemblances between the international League
and the British Commonwealth of Nations did not signify that these
two political organizations were incompatible or even competitive
with one another. On the contrary, they were not only mutually
helpful but perhaps mutually indispensable. The Commonwealth ✓
lightened the task of the League in several ways—for example, by
taking off its shoulders large parts of the two awkward problems of
migration and of the contact of civilizations, and by serving in some
sense as a buffer between the League and one of the two Great Powers
which had remained outside it, in virtue of the close geographical and
economic relations of Canada and the strong sentimental relations of
Ireland with the United States. On the other side, the League was
of inestimable value to the Commonwealth as a scheme of partial
insurance against another outbreak of international (and hence-
forward almost *ex hypothesi* world-wide) war.

For the British Commonwealth in this delicate stage of its evolution
this contingency was the crucial danger. The ' Chanāq Incident '[2]
had shown that it was not enough for the security of the Commonwealth that war should be outlawed as between the states members
of the Commonwealth themselves. It had given warning of the
severity of the strain which would be thrown upon the unity of the
Commonwealth by anything like a repetition of those events which,
in 1914, had automatically placed the self-governing Dominions of
the British Empire in a state of ' passive ' belligerency with a foreign

[1] See Section (ii) below.   [2] See Section (ii) below.

state. It could not be taken for granted that, if that situation were
to recur, all the self-governing communities in the Empire would
decide again to translate their belligerency into active terms ; and,
if one or more of them were to refrain from doing so, it could not be
guaranteed that the unity of the Empire would be preserved. Therefore, it was one of the capital interests of the British Commonwealth
(for which the prospect of another outbreak of international war thus
involved the menace, not merely of some loss of territory, trade, or
prestige, but of actual dissolution) that the danger of international
war should be reduced to a minimum—a result which could only be
brought about by some international organization, and which was
in fact the aim of the League. It is true that in 1926 (as has been
mentioned already) this aim of the League had by no means been
attained. ' The gap in the Covenant ' had not yet been closed, and
two out of the surviving seven Great Powers in the world had not
become League members. In consequence, the Sword of Damocles
still remained suspended over the British Commonwealth's head ;
and indeed it might be argued that the states members of the Commonwealth had exposed themselves to a new danger by undertaking
the obligations of Article 16 of the Covenant when the performance
of these obligations—raising, as it would do, the controversial
question of the interpretation of maritime law—might bring them
into collision with the United States. Yet though the League had
not yet succeeded in making the outlawry of international war complete, the existence and constitution of the League already ensured
that if, in spite of the League machinery, another international war
were to break out, the strain upon the cohesion of the British Commonwealth would be less severe, in one important respect, than if
the League had not existed and if all states members of the Commonwealth had not, in their own rights, become League members likewise. This safeguard consisted in the fact that the League possessed
a written constitution under which, in the event of war, the respective
and mutual obligations of states members of the League were to a
large extent predetermined. Thus, if another international war were
to break out, the states members of the British Commonwealth
would probably find their respective and mutual obligations determined for them in their quality as members of the League, and would
thus be released from the predicament of having to determine their
obligations as states members of the Commonwealth.[1]

[1] For an exposition of this point see Professor A. F. Pollard, *The Dominions
and Foreign Affairs* (paper read at a meeting of the British Institute of
International Affairs on the 24th May, 1921), p. 13.

Indeed, the existence of a written constitution in the organization
of an international League of which the self-governing British communities were each severally members removed the principal objection to the absence of a written constitution in the organization of
the British Commonwealth, and so dispensed British statesmen from
putting their necks under a yoke which they instinctively and
traditionally abhorred.   Possibly they were all the more sensitive
to the irksomeness of such a yoke because, on at least two occasions
within the previous ten years, they had almost fallen under it.

The first occasion had been the Imperial War Conference of 1917,
at which a resolution had been adopted containing a paragraph to
the effect that, in the opinion of the Conference, the readjustment
of the constitutional relations of the component parts of the Empire,
being too important and intricate a subject to be dealt with during
the War, should form the subject of a special Imperial Conference to
be summoned as soon as possible after the cessation of hostilities.   At
the Imperial Conference of 1921, however, the British Prime Minister,
Mr. Lloyd George, found it desirable to mention, in order to repudiate, a rumour that His Majesty's Government in Great Britain were
' dissatisfied with the present state of the Empire ' and wished ' to
alter its organization in some revolutionary way ' ;   the Canadian
Prime Minister, Mr. Meighen, disowned any such suspicion as far as
any responsible representative of Canada was concerned ; while the
Australian Prime Minister, Mr. Hughes, declared himself ' totally at
a loss to understand ' what it was that the Constitutional Conference
which had been contemplated in the Resolution of 1917 proposed to
do, and—on the assumption that it was not intended to limit those
rights which the Dominions already possessed—asked what new right
or what extension of power such a conference could give to them.[1]
In fine, at the Imperial Conference of 1921, ' the surprising conclusion
was reached ' that the Constitutional Conference was no longer
necessary ; [2] and the proposal was finally disposed of when the
' opinion that nothing would be gained by attempting to lay down
a constitution for the British Empire ' was recorded in the Report of
the Inter-Imperial Relations Committee of 1926.[3]

The second occasion when the yoke of a written constitution
threatened to descend upon British statesmen's necks was the negotiation of the Irish Agreement in 1921, since the common ground from

[1] For the foregoing references to the ' Constitutional Conference ', which
were all made in the opening speeches of the 1921 Conference, on the 20th June,
1921, see *Cmd.* 1474 of 1921, pp. 14, 17, and 22.
[2] Sir Robert Borden, *op. cit.*
[3] *Cmd.* 2768 of 1926, p. 14.

which the negotiators started was that Ireland was to become a self-governing Dominion of the British Commonwealth with a title to most-favoured-Dominion treatment, and the Irish negotiators—for whom the British Commonwealth was as yet no more than a name to which there was little that corresponded in the Irish experience of the British Empire—naturally desired that this 'Dominion Status' should be defined in terms. The British negotiators, however, successfully resisted the inclusion in the Agreement of any definition of 'Dominion Status' except by reference to the concrete instance of Canada, and left it to those Irish statesmen who subsequently drafted the Constitution of the Irish Free State to work out in precise detail what the full implications of this reference were—His Majesty's Government in Great Britain committing itself, even then, to nothing beyond an intimation that, in their opinion, the terms of the Free State Constitution, as submitted to the Parliament at Westminster for its approval, were not contrary to the terms of the Agreement.

Such, in 1926, was 'the British Commonwealth of Nations'. It was a new political 'mutation' within the British Empire, in virtue of which the British Empire, 'considered as a whole', had become a 'political organization' that 'defied classification' and bore 'no real resemblance' to any other. The only political phenomenon in the contemporary world that displayed points of resemblance to the British Commonwealth was the equally new-fangled international League (inasmuch as 'free co-operation' was 'the instrument' of both alike) ; and the Commonwealth differed notably even from the League in the fact that it was governed, not by a Covenant, but 'by an unwritten treaty of mutual guarantee'.[1] The Inter-Imperial Relations Committee of 1926, after writing into their report that definition of the Commonwealth which has been quoted above,[2] immediately went on to observe that 'a foreigner endeavouring to understand the true character of the British Empire by the aid of this formula alone would be tempted to think that it was devised rather to make mutual interference impossible than to make mutual co-operation easy'. Yet they boldly expressed the opinion that though every Dominion was then, and must always remain, 'the sole judge of the nature and extent of its co-operation, no common cause' would 'be thereby imperilled' ; and their boldness was well grounded, since this free and informal 'Commonwealth of Nations' —to Americans a stumbling-block, to Europeans folly—was the

[1] Phrase used by Mr. Bruce in a speech delivered in the Australian Parliament on the 3rd August, 1926 (*The Times*, 4th August, 1926).

[2] See p. 16 above.

mature fruit of British statesmanship, ripened by the cumulative experience of many generations.

What was it, then, which instilled into the minds of the statesmen of the Commonwealth that strong, and apparently not diminishing, reluctance to commit this precious heritage of political wisdom to writing ? The hypothetical foreign investigator would be reminded, it may be, of the similar aversion of famous prophets and philosophers from the written word, and would surmise (if charitably inclined) that Mr. Bruce, like Plato, was convinced that the esoteric mystery of his faith would be distorted and desecrated by the gross medium of ink and paper, or else (in an uncharitable mood) that these professed statesmen were impostors and all their discourse, with its new-fangled terms, no more than ' sounding brass and tinkling cymbals ' naïvely devised in order to give the dissolution of an Empire *in articulo mortis* the appearance of a euthanasia. Yet, however pardonably he might be tempted so to think, the hypothetical foreigner would have been wrong, as a study of Mr. Bruce's oral instruction will show.

> It would be disastrous [Mr. Bruce declared in his opening speech at the Imperial Conference of 1926] to attempt to lay down something in the nature of a written constitution that is going to govern us in the future. It is quite impossible for an Empire progressing continually, as we are, to have such a document. If we had had it in the past, either it would have had to be torn up or it would have destroyed the Empire.[1]

The statesmen of the British Commonwealth, who would have disavowed the role of either prophets or impostors with almost equal distaste, flattered themselves that they were ' practical men ' ; and their wisdom consisted in a timely discernment and acceptance of accomplished facts in a changing world.

Sometimes, with the perversity of ' practical men ', they had elected to be only just in time ; and more than once this weakness had been dearly paid for. In both Canada and Ireland ' Dominion Status ' had followed and not forestalled a national insurrection against the British Empire ; in South Africa it had followed and not forestalled an international war. In Ireland, above all, salvation had been bought—after a riot of destruction, misery, and humiliation—at the eleventh hour. Yet the British statesmen who affected this sluggish gait never forgot that on one fatal occasion—the first on which the problem of evolving the Commonwealth out of the Empire

---

[1] *Cmd.* 2769 of 1927, p. 19. Compare an almost identical passage in a public statement made by Mr. Bruce on the day of his arrival in London, the 11th October, 1926 (*The Times,* 12th October, 1926).

arose—their predecessors had altogether missed the tide. Between
1783 and 1926, that supreme and irreparable mistake, at any rate,
had not been committed again ; and on a broad view the vital matter
was that—whether on the full flood or on the last waves of an ebbing
tide—the ship of state in each community of the Empire, as it
became capable of Dominion Status, should be safely launched and
guided out to sea. On behalf of British statesmanship it may be
submitted that the right perspective in which to view its good and
its evil deeds, its successes and its failures, during the century and
a half preceding the Imperial Conference of 1926, would be found in
a comparison of the fortunes of the British Empire, from beginning
to end of this period, with those of the other Empires which were its
contemporaries in age and its peers in the rank of ' Great Powers '.
The lesson which had been learnt, once for all, by British statesmen
before the American War of Independence came to an end had not
been learnt by the statesmen of the three ' Great Powers ' of Eastern
Europe—the Empires of the Hohenzollern, Hapsburg, and Romanov
Dynasties—before the outbreak of the General War of 1914–18 ; and
therefore, when the tempest caught them, they were driven help-
lessly, one after another, to shipwreck on a lee shore, while the
British Empire—re-rigged in time with an eye to heavy weather—
successfully rode the storm.

Moreover, the British habit of ' being only just in time ', though
it had been responsible for some political tragedies for which atone-
ment and reparation were not easily made, had also certain ' practical ' advantages to commend it. It was a guarantee that the gradual
and piecemeal evolution of the Commonwealth out of the Empire,
while never retarded to the point of irretrievable disaster, should not
on the other hand be exposed to possibilities of disaster at least as
grave by being prematurely pressed forward.[1] To be ' in time but
only just in time' made it possible to practise a thoroughly empirical
statesmanship, without prepossessions but also without prejudices ;
and it was perhaps because they were animated by this temper that
British statesmen steadily continued to discern and accept accomplished facts in a world that was now changing so fast that some of
the political developments in it were unprecedented. Since (as has

---

[1] In 1926 there were several parts of the Empire—e. g. India, Kenya, and
Southern Rhodesia among others—in which the possibility of disaster, if the
pace were forced, was evident. Even in the cases of Canada and South Africa,
in which the verdict of history might be that the British Government had
procrastinated unduly, it has to be remembered on the other side how young
and tender a growth the nationhood of Canada was in 1867 and the nationhood of South Africa in 1910.

been recalled above) the British Empire at this time was an almost
complete sample of contemporary human society, it was evidently
necessary for the salvation of the Empire that its statesmen should
be ready to ' live perilously ' and to make use of all their accumulated
lore for cautiously steering, where occasion required it, an uncharted
course ; and in such necessary but dangerous enterprises of political
exploration their empirical habit of mind stood them in good stead.

It may be well to conclude this introduction by setting out briefly
the chief of those world-wide changes which were in progress at the
time and then noting, in each case, the manner in which the British
Empire was attempting to adapt itself to a changing environment
through the progressive evolution of the British Commonwealth in
response to the new problems as they successively arose.

(i) *The fundamental change, of which the others were corollaries, was
that the international system to which the British Empire belonged had
ceased to be a European system with overseas appendages and had become
a world-wide system in which Europe no longer retained a predominance.*
This momentous change (a new departure from an international
system which had been consistently Europo-centric for four centuries)
was eloquently described by General Smuts in the opening speech
which he delivered on the 20th June, 1921, at the first sitting of the
Imperial Conference of that year.

In shaping our course for the future, we must bear in mind that the
whole world position has radically altered as a result of the War.
Europe is no longer what she was, and the power and the position which
she once occupied in the world has been largely lost. The great Empires
have disappeared. Austria will never rise again. Russia and Germany
will no doubt revive, but not in this generation nor in the next ; and
when they do, they may be very different countries in a world which
may be a very different world. The position, therefore, has completely
altered. The old viewpoint from which we considered Europe has completely altered. She suffers from an exhaustion which is the most
appalling fact of history ; and the victorious countries of Europe are
not much better off than the vanquished. No, the scene has shifted on
the great stage. To my mind that is the most important fact in the
world situation to-day, and the fact to which our foreign policy should
have special regard. Our temptation is still to look upon the European
stage as of the first importance. It is no longer so ; and I suggest we
should not be too deeply occupied with it. Let us be friendly and helpful all round to the best of our ability, but let us not be too deeply involved in it. The fires are still burning there, the pot is occasionally
boiling over, but these are not really first-rate events any more. The
state of affairs in central Europe will probably continue for many years
to come, and no act on our part could very largely alter the situation.
Therefore, not from feelings of selfishness, but in a spirit of wisdom, one

would counsel prudence and reserve in our Continental commitments, and that we do not let ourselves in for European entanglements more than is necessary, and that we be impartial, friendly, and helpful to all alike, and avoid any partisan attitude in the concerns of the continent of Europe. Undoubtedly the scene has shifted away from Europe to the Far East and to the Pacific. The problems of the Pacific are to my mind the world problems of the next fifty years or more. In these problems we are, as an Empire, very vitally interested. Three of the Dominions border on the Pacific ; India is next door ; there, too, are the United States and Japan. There, also, in China, the fate of the greatest human population on earth will have to be decided. There Europe, Asia, and America are meeting, and there, I believe, the next great chapter in human history will be enacted. I ask myself what will be the character of that history ? Will it be along the old lines ? Will it be the old spirit of national and imperial domination which has been the undoing of Europe ? Or shall we have learned our lesson ? Shall we have purged our souls in the fires through which we have passed ? Will it be a future of peaceful co-operation, of friendly co-ordination of all the vast interests at stake ? [1]

During the half-century that followed the battle of Waterloo— the formative period of ' Dominion Status ' as it evolved out of the relations of Great Britain with the British Dominions of European origin overseas—the peoples of Continental Europe had been re- cuperating from the exhausting effects of the General War of 1792– 1815 and preoccupied with the immediate task of undoing the posi- tive work of the Peace Settlement of Vienna.[2] They had therefore submitted to the temporary insulation of the overseas world from the European Continent through the exercise of an undisputed ascen- dancy by the British Navy—a British ' thalassocracy ' which, as the physical sanction behind the ' Monroe Doctrine ' of the United States, created the opportunity for the firm establishment of national self- government not only in the British but in the former Spanish and Portuguese dominions of European origin overseas and thereby truly ' called a New World into existence to redress the balance of the Old '. This insulation had only lasted for half a century ; but the psychological effect upon the nascent nations overseas was so pro- found that it was still prevalent when the next General War broke out in 1914.

We had been too busily engaged [declared an Australian statesman in retrospect] [3] in trying to develop our own countries, in carrying out

[1] *Cmd.* 1474 of 1921, p. 25.

[2] The negative achievement of the Vienna Congress was the liquidation of the Napoleonic Empire, and that achievement, of course, was permanent.

[3] Speech delivered by Mr. Bruce to the United States Pilgrims' Association at New York on the 29th December, 1926 (Text in *International Concilia- tion*, No. 228).

our own social experiments, in trying our new systems of government, and we had forgotten there was an outside world. We had forgotten that there were great complications that could come to us from that outside world.

During the following period, which lasted from the end of the third quarter of the nineteenth century until the outbreak of the General War of 1914–18, these complications had begun to reappear ; for in the ' eighties ' and ' nineties ' the Continental European peoples, having tardily succeeded in arranging their domestic affairs, had started once more to stretch out their hands across the sea ; and this renewal of Continental European expansion had begun—at least in certain regions overseas such as Tropical Africa or the Far East and the Pacific—to complicate the conduct of the inter-Imperial affairs of the British Empire by weaving them once again into that system of international relations from which they had been virtually insulated for more than fifty years. Finally, since the General War of 1914–18, this non-European world—in which lay scattered the whole of the British Empire except the British Isles—had become so deeply implicated in the plot of the international drama that (as General Smuts pointed out in 1921) [1] the main action in the next scene seemed likely to be performed on a non-European part of the world-stage.

It was true that the War had checked the tendency of the last half-century for Continental European Powers to intervene in non-European affairs and to this extent had restored the situation of the half-century ending in 1871, during which the overseas world had been able to work out special solutions for its special problems in a state of virtual insulation from European affairs ; but this second release of the overseas world from the operation of Continental European forces, which followed the General War of 1914–18, unlike the first release which had followed the General War of 1792–1815, did not bring with it a total exemption from the entanglement of international affairs, since the War of 1914–18 had been followed also by a transference of the centre of gravity of the international system into the overseas world itself. The extent of this transference may be measured by the change in the distribution of the principal pieces on the board. Of the eight Great Powers which existed in the world in August 1914, four (Germany, France, the Hapsburg Monarchy, and Italy) had been wholly based on European ground ; two (the British and the Russian Empires) had had their bases partly in Europe and partly outside it ; and only two (the United States and Japan) had

---

[1] See p. 30 above.

been wholly non-European. Of the three Great Powers with world-wide interests (the British Empire, the United States, and the U.S.S.R.) which emerged from the War of 1914–18, not one was wholly based on European ground and only one out of the three (the British Empire) had any footing in Europe at all—the United States having remained wholly non-European and the U.S.S.R. (in contrast to the former Russian Empire) having become so. It was only among the three surviving Great Powers whose interests were less than world-wide (namely Japan, France, and Italy) that Europe could still show a majority.

The response, in the constitutional development of the British Empire, to this new change in the world position was the recognition of a parity of status between the non-European self-governing Do-minions overseas and the European ' nerve-centre ' of the Empire, Great Britain, without prejudice to that common allegiance to the Crown which made it possible for the communities of an Empire represented in every quarter of a now unified world to maintain a united front in their foreign relations.

(ii) *The second change in the world-position was that the world as a whole had become what only Europe had been before, that is, a one and indivisible field of international action*; and this point, again, was vividly presented, in an address to an American audience, by one of the statesmen of the British Commonwealth, the Australian Prime Minister, Mr. Bruce.[1]

> We have had an astounding lesson that the world has become smaller with the advance of science, with the development of modern inventions and modern transport, in the position in which we all found ourselves in the War. We, in Australia, imagined that wars could take place in Europe and we could go on with our great task of development. We found we were wrong. So the whole world has found.

The response, within the British Empire, to this second change in the world as a whole was to be seen in the efforts, made since the termination of the General War of 1914–18, to provide for a more effective co-operation between the several states members of the Commonwealth in arrangements for Imperial defence and in the con-duct of foreign relations.

The problem of co-operation in the conduct of foreign relations was peculiarly difficult at this time by reason of the particular stage which had been reached in the progress of the new technique for the navigation of the air—a striking illustration of the fact that for the

[1] Speech delivered on the 29th December, 1926, at New York to the United States Pilgrims' Association (reprinted in *International Conciliation*, No. 228 ; see p. 143.)

British Empire, as a complete sample of contemporary human society, hardly anything was immaterial that fell within the field of human affairs.[1] As has been mentioned above, the new mastery of the air and the new increase in the potency of heavy artillery had already brought Great Britain within effective range of the European Continent on the strategic plane, and had thereby created a greater difference between the respective strategic situations of Great Britain and the overseas Dominions than had existed before. The essential safeguard against this new danger to the unity of the Empire was that, in all matters of Imperial foreign relations which involved the issues of peace and war, there should be a corresponding increase of co-operation between the responsible authorities in the several states members of the Commonwealth. This proposition was indeed regarded as self-evident on all hands ; and it was further agreed that, as between self-governing countries in which the system of responsible parliamentary Government was in force, the responsible authorities through whom the co-operation was to be maintained must be the respective Prime Ministers themselves. In the third place, it was agreed that communication by dispatch and telegram, however efficiently organized, was a *pis aller* which could never become a full and sufficient substitute for personal contact; and that personal meetings between Prime Ministers would not be rendered superfluous even by the establishment of a permanent two-way personal contact through the adoption, by the Governments of states members of the Commonwealth, of some system of personal representation in one another's capitals, on the analogy of the reciprocal diplomatic representation which had been customary for many centuries in the relations between sovereign independent states. It followed that periodical Imperial Conferences of Prime Ministers were and would continue to be indispensable, and that, the more often they were held, the more effective the safeguard to Imperial unity would be ; but here the statesmanship of the Empire was confronted with the practical difficulty that the progress of aviation, which had made the problem of the co-ordination of Imperial foreign policy more acute by threatening to turn Great Britain, on the strategic plane, into an integral part of the European Continent, had not yet advanced sufficiently to provide the natural solution for the difficulty which it had created. Eventually, it was to be hoped that the progress of aviation would make it possible to travel between London and Ottawa, between London and Pretoria, and even between London and Delhi, Canberra,

---

[1] ' Nihil humanum a me alienum puto ' might have served as the motto of the British Empire at this stage of its history.

or Wellington as rapidly and easily as it was possible already to
travel by train and steamship between Geneva and Paris, London,
Berlin, or Rome. In 1926, however, this consummation of progress
in the mastery of the air was hardly yet in prospect—notwithstanding the joint and several efforts for the opening up of British Imperial
air-ways on which the self-governing communities of the Empire had
been engaged since the termination of the War—and in the meantime
the Prime Ministers (with no more rapid means of personal communication yet at their disposal than the old-fashioned steamship and
railroad) were finding it more and more difficult to reconcile the
prolonged absences from home which were thus still necessitated by
Imperial Conferences with the more and more exacting duties of the
Prime Minister's office in countries, enjoying responsible parliamentary government, which were growing in political stature year by
year. This practical difficulty of course presented itself in its most
acute form to the Prime Ministers of New Zealand and Australia ;
and at the Imperial Conference of 1921 both Mr. Massey and
Mr. Hughes laid great stress upon it.[1]   Indeed, this was one reason
(though of course not the only reason) for the lapse of the resolution,
taken by the Imperial War Conference in 1917, to hold a Constitutional Conference after peace had been restored,[2] and for the non-
pursuance of the suggestion which was made on the 23rd and the 25th
June, 1924, by His Majesty's Government in Great Britain to the
Governments of the other states members of the Commonwealth
that the problems involved in consultation on matters of foreign
policy and of general Imperial interest should be subjected to a
common examination, of a preliminary character, at a meeting to
be held immediately after the forthcoming session of the Assembly
of the League of Nations.[3]

(iii) *The third change in the world to which the British Empire had to
adapt itself was the ferment which the leaven of Western civilization was
producing in all mankind*—a change depicted by General Smuts, in
1918, in the arresting metaphor that ' the tents have been struck
and the great caravan of Humanity is once more on the march '.   On
the political plane,[4] a body of ideas which had been generated by the
evolution of responsible parliamentary government in Great Britain
and in her daughter-countries overseas, was pressing further forward

---

[1] See *Cmd.* 1474 of 1921, pp. 18–19 and 27–8.
[2] On this point, see Mr. Massey's remark, reported in *Cmd.* 1474 of 1921,
p. 27.
[3] See *The Times*, 9th January, 1925, and Section (v) (*a*) below.
[4] The political plane, of course, was superficial by comparison with the
economic and the cultural planes, on which the ferment was also at work.

in its triumphal progress through the world.[1]   At the close of the
eighteenth century this movement—started by the constitutional
evolution of Great Britain herself and modified by the revolution in
the Thirteen Colonies—had invaded France, and thence, in a French
adaptation, it had pushed on into Central and Eastern Europe.   Its
definitive victory there was proclaimed by the downfall of the three
Dynastic Empires in the General War of 1914–18 and by the emergence, from among their ruins, of a number of ' successor states '
professedly founded on the principles of Nationality and Democracy.
By 1926, before the imagination of mankind had fully comprehended
the significance of this transformation of the European scene, the
movement was already sweeping on again from Continental Europe
into the Islamic World ; and Angora and Damascus and Kabul were
being rudely awakened from a long political slumber by the Principles
of the French Revolution—long since a platitude in the West, but
still a trumpet-call in unaccustomed ears.[2]   Simultaneously the same
movement, in its American form, was producing a ferment in the
Philippines ; [3] and in its British form it was radiating from its
original starting-point in Great Britain and the Dominions of
European origin overseas to one after another of the remaining communities in the British Empire—to old European communities like
those in Southern Ireland and in Cyprus, to old Asiatic communities
like those in India and in Ceylon, and to such special creations of the
British Empire itself as Malta and Southern Rhodesia.

The response of British statesmanship to this world-wide fermentation, of which the leaven had come, in the first instance, from Great
Britain itself, was a deliberate resolution to enter upon a new departure in policy in regard to the conferment of Dominion Status—a
voyage of political exploration which was justified by the evident

---

[1] It might be contended that while this body of political ideas was gaining
ground in some quarters it was losing it in others, e. g. in Italy, where it had
been introduced in the Risorgimento only to be rejected in the Fascist Movement.   In regard to this two observations may be made.   In the first place, this
body of political ideas had two aspects—Democracy and Nationality—and
while the Fascisti were in reaction against Democracy they were devotees
to Nationality.   In the second place, the phenomenon of the dictatorship,
which had appeared, since the termination of the General War of 1914–18,
not only in Italy but in other Western communities—for example, Spain,
Bavaria, Hungary, and Poland—as well as in China, Russia, Bulgaria, Greece,
and the Islamic World, was likely, according to all historical precedents, to
be ephemeral.   It had the appearance of a temporary pathological symptom
resulting from overstrain, rather than of a new departure in political ideas
with an important future.

[2] See *Survey for 1925*, vol. i, Introduction.

[3] See *Survey for 1926*, Part III B, Section (iv).

fact that such an Empire in such a world must dare ' to live perilously ' if it was to save its soul alive.

Hitherto—and it was well for the British people to confess this in all humility, in order that they might escape the envy of the gods—the evolution of Dominion Status had been carried on under exceptionally favourable conditions. The communities on which, so far, this status had been successfully conferred were all of them young communities of European origin overseas, and that was evidently the best environment in which this new political experiment could be made. Owing to their wholly European and largely British origin, these communities possessed a social heritage which made it almost their second nature to exercise those political aptitudes which the enjoyment of Dominion Status presupposed ; while, owing to their youth and to their being bedded out on virgin soil in a sheltered situation, they were distinguished—in politics as in the other functions of social life—by an unusual plasticity which made them admirable vehicles for the first essay in a new ' variation ' or ' mutation ' in political structure.

One conspicuous evidence of this plasticity was the rapidity with which even the bitterest memories were obliterated from the minds of these young communities overseas by the absorbing interest of that ' great task of development ' [1] which was a perpetual incentive to co-operation for all their citizens. Hence, in these fortunate communities, spiritual wounds which might have proved incurable in the mental atmosphere of the Old World frequently healed, almost of themselves, before they had time to fester. In North America French-speaking and English-speaking Canadians found it far easier to grow together into a single nation than it was found in Europe by French-speaking and Flemish-speaking Belgians ; and in South Africa a particular international situation which had produced a world-wide catastrophe when it afterwards arose in Europe had been met and transcended at the cost of far less suffering and destruction.[2] The overseas atmosphere was the more potent for

[1] Mr. Bruce at New York, 29th December, 1926.
[2] The essence of the situation was that a nationality (the Jugoslavs in the one case, the Afrikanders in the other) which desired political unity without the sacrifice of self-government, found itself partitioned politically between a multi-national state (the Hapsburg Monarchy in the one case, the British Empire in the other) in which it was not itself the dominant nationality, and two small independent states (Serbia and Montenegro in the one case and the Transvaal and the Orange Free State in the other). When this situation arose in Europe as between the Hapsburg Monarchy and the Jugoslavs, it resulted in the destruction of a Great Power during the convulsions of a General War and in the satisfaction of the principle of Nationality by a revolutionary

good inasmuch as it produced its effect, not only upon the overseas communities themselves, but upon those statesmen in Great Britain upon whose outlook and action the evolution of relations between the Dominions and the Mother Country in its earlier stages chiefly depended for good or evil. The importance, for the evolution of Dominion Status in its original overseas environment, of this influence of the overseas spirit upon statesmanship in Whitehall can be gauged by the extraordinary contrast between the large-minded generosity of the Quebec Act of 1774—an act which laid the foundations of a friendship between the conquered French settlers in North America and the victorious Empire which was the hereditary enemy of their Mother Country in Europe—and the ferocity of the anti-Catholic laws which the same British Government kept on the statute book in Ireland until 1829.

After the War of 1914–18 British statesmanship addressed itself —not with alacrity or with a light heart, but in obedience to its empirical habit of discerning and accepting accomplished facts at the eleventh hour—to the new and hazardous but imperative task of conferring the new institution of Dominion Status, which had just been evolved in the unusually favourable environment of the overseas world, upon communities in the Empire among whom the conditions under which the experiment must be tried were distinctly adverse in more than one respect—not only on account of the social heritages of these communities but on account of their relations with Great Britain, and their position in the British Empire, in the immediate past.

One of these communities lay in Ireland—a country which, in spite of its geographical situation on the extreme oceanic verge of Europe, reaching out towards the New World, had been oppressed by a political atmosphere utterly different from that overseas atmosphere in which Dominion Status had originally taken form. Whereas the secret of the political strength of the overseas peoples lay in a happy capacity, induced by the environment, for forgetting the past, it was pertinently remarked by Mr. Lloyd George, during the negotiation of the Irish Agreement in 1921, that ' in Ireland there is no past ; it is all present '. This almost pathological inability to forget a wrong after it had ceased to be inflicted was, of course, not

change at an immoderate cost. When it arose overseas between the British Empire and the Afrikanders, it resulted in the satisfaction of the same principle of Nationality after a local war which, instead of proving an irreparable calamity, was followed by the evolution of a South African Union endowed with Dominion Status as a state member of the British Commonwealth of Nations.

peculiar to the Irish people. It was characteristic of all peoples who, instead of growing up, like the overseas communities, on virgin soil, had been condemned by Fate to go on living upon fields sown with dragon's teeth and watered with blood. The self-same habit of mind that had been induced in the Irish by successive oppressions at the hands of Scandinavian, Norman, and English invaders and conquerors, had been induced in Slavs and Greeks by similar sufferings at the hands of Huns and Crusaders and Turks, with the result that, in the first quarter of the twentieth century, an English observer who was acquainted with the atmosphere of South-Eastern Europe at first hand was able to apprehend the atmosphere of Ireland by analogy, and *vice versa*. It will appear from this how much more formidable a task the inauguration of Dominion Status was in Ireland in 1921 than it had been in Canada in 1867 or even in South Africa in 1910.

Another community in which the experiment of Dominion Status had likewise to be initiated at the same time was India—a country where memories as baleful as any that haunted Ireland were set hard in a religious mould and therefore threatened to offer a still tougher obstruction to political growth—even though, in this case, the ancient wrongs by which the brooding spirit had been generated had been the work of conquerors whose bones had turned to dust long before the first Englishman set foot on those shores. In India, moreover, the inability to forget was far from being the only obstacle to the success of the new enterprise ; and those Indians and Englishmen who co-operated in the drafting and the working of the Government of India Act of 1919 had simultaneously to contend with the vast size of the country, the vast number, poverty, and illiteracy of its inhabitants, and the multiplicity and sharpness of the racial, linguistic, religious, and social barriers which divided them—and that by gulfs so difficult to pass that it might be said, without extravagance, that the only common feature in their manifold social heritages was a uniform absence of that kind of political experience and tradition out of which the institution of responsible parliamentary government had originally grown on its native British soil.

The creation of a new self-governing Dominion through the establishment of the Irish Free State and the evolution of another new self-governing Dominion through the working of the Government of India Act were the two principal enterprises on which the statesmanship of the British Empire was at that time engaged. It was success or failure in these two fields that would decide whether or not the evolution of the British Commonwealth within the British

Empire was to go forward until the parent organization had been wholly absorbed into and transfigured by the new creature to which it had given life. The same alternative would probably determine the verdict of history upon the political achievement of the British people, who would be judged, according to the event, either to have been endowed with an almost unparalleled genius for constructive statesmanship or else to have reaped a cheap and transitory reputation from a few local successes in which the credit for the goodness of the crop was evidently due to the virginity of the soil rather than to the skill of the husbandman. Yet at a time when two enterprises fraught with such momentous issues were heavy on their hands, the statesmen of the Empire found leisure and energy to carry forward the evolution of the Commonwealth on a number of subsidiary fields by erecting Southern Rhodesia into a self-governing colony, introducing a system of 'dyarchy' in Malta, granting majorities of elected members in colonial councils and assemblies, and inaugurating other constitutional developments, in Ceylon and other Crown Colonies and Protectorates, and presiding over a constitutional reorganization in the Federated Malay States.

If this grand experiment were miraculously to succeed, there was little danger that the final result would be (as was sometimes prophesied) a dull uniformity in which ubiquitous reproductions of the British Constitution would take the colour and variety out of a muffled world. On the contrary, even at this early stage in the evolution of the British Commonwealth, it was already evident that the application of identical principles, when adapted, by the empirical British method of trial and error, to the local conditions of the various social environments in which the experiment was being carried on, would make the British Commonwealth at the end of the process a still more highly diversified political organization than the British Empire had been at the beginning.

Canada and Australia would probably grow into communities of the same stature and species as the United States,[1] New Zealand

[1] ' Between the United States and my own country there are many points of contact. We rightly or wrongly look toward America as the realization of many of those things we set before ourselves when we are visualizing the great destiny that we are confident will be our portion in the years to come. It is only a hundred years ago that this great nation of yours, which is the admiration of the world, was a small people with a great task similar to that which confronts Australia and its small population to-day. I can only say that we draw inspiration from what you have accomplished, but we have a great belief in our own country, a great confidence in ourselves.' (Mr. Bruce at New York, 29th December, 1926.) The last sentence in this quotation suggests that the specific resemblance of Australia to the United States would not

into an antipodean counterpart of Great Britain, while the range of potentialities in the destiny of South Africa was extraordinarily wide. On the one hand, the Union might decide to restrict its area to territories which were capable of being made into ' a White Man's country ' and might make it its paramount aim to keep the proportion of Whites to Blacks in the population as high as possible— even if it were recognized that the policy of ' segregation ' could never be carried to the logical conclusion of shaping the Union into a wholly White enclave in a Black continent. On the other hand, if the original union of four provinces in South Africa followed the example of the original union of thirteen states on the east coast of North America by expanding into the interior of the continent, it might grow into a vast federal state extending from the Cape to the Equator —an African counterpart of Brazil in the Southern Hemisphere and of India in the Northern. If that proved to be the South Africans' destiny, they would almost certainly have to pay for it, sooner or later, by the sacrifice of the ' White South Africa ' ideal ; [1] and in that event it would make little practical difference in the long run whether, like the Hindus, they set up the institution of caste as their

extend to details, and indeed it was probable, on the face of it, that the farther Australia and the other self-governing Dominions of the British Empire developed, the more strongly pronounced would become their national individuality. Psychologically, not only Australia but Canada—which was linked up with the United States by much closer geographical and economic ties—had already evolved a distinctive national type. The approximation of Canada and Australia to the United States was greatest, perhaps, in the social and commercial spheres and in the general structure of political institutions, while in political practice and in legal and educational matters there was a certain tendency towards differentiation. At the same time, it was to be expected that a powerful standardizing influence would be exerted by the expansion of American trade and American capital investment—an expansion which had long been at work in Canada and which was beginning, in 1926, to make itself felt in Australia also.

[1] At the time of writing, the factor which was chiefly hindering the expansion of the Union of South Africa towards the Equator was not a fear, on the part of the South Africans, that the Black population of Central Africa might upset the balance in the Union between Black and White, but rather a fear, on the part of the White settlers in Rhodesia and East Africa, who were predominantly English-speaking people of British origin, that federation with the Union would commit them to an English-Afrikaans bilingualism in administration and education. The dislike of this possible consequence of adhesion to the Union was apparently stronger than the desire, which these tiny White minorities in Central and East Africa also felt, to strengthen their position against the Black majorities among whom they lived by drawing closer to the one considerable body of White population on the Continent. Thus the minor and probably ephemeral conflict between the English and the Dutch nationality within the bosom of the White community in Africa still counted for more than the deeper and in all probability longer enduring division between the White and Black races.

monument to a desperate attempt to resist miscegenation, or whether, like the Brazilians, they joyously abandoned themselves to the cult of the Goddess Pammixia. As for India, her destiny pointed to her becoming the representative, within the British Commonwealth, of an Oriental type of United States which would be represented in the world at large by the U.S.S.R. and China. At the opposite extremity of the territorial scale, the embryonic city-states of Hongkong and the Straits Settlements were bidding for a commercial hegemony in the Pacific not unlike that which had been exercised in the Mediterranean, in certain past ages, by Venice and by Rhodes.[1] Other British colonies and protectorates in the tropical belt—in Malaya, the West Indies, and West Africa—might look forward to being taken up from the Empire into the Commonwealth through some solution of the problem (which also confronted the United States in the Philippines) of finding in tropical agriculture the economic basis, not for an oligarchy of alien planters, but for a native freeholding peasantry. In the Irish Free State an ancient European nation might at last satisfy a desire for national self-expression, too long frustrated, by an archaistic revival of the kind to which the new 'Successor States' in Central and Eastern Europe were devoting part of their energies. The Falkland Islands might become an antipodean Iceland—evoking once again, by the challenge of a stern environment, the highest qualities of 'Nordic Man'.

(iv) *A fourth change in the world to which the British Empire had to adapt itself*—and it was here, perhaps, that the principle latent in the structure of the Commonwealth had the greatest service to render to mankind—*was the great change for the worse which had recently come over the institution of War.* In previous ages War had been an offence against civilization which could sometimes be committed without fatal results, because it had been possible to fight 'limited wars' in which not all the sovereign independent states in the world were engaged and in which even the belligerent states did not stake the whole of their wealth or hazard the lives of all their citizens. The General War of 1914–18 had given warning that the days of such 'limited wars' were drawing to a close, and that, at the pitch to which technique and organization were being developed by the persevering ingenuity of Western man, it would become less and less possible for war to be waged in future without engaging the

[1] To the same category belonged the International Settlement of Shanghai, with its highly developed municipal administration, which had been built up mainly by British residents, though the settlement never had formed and was not likely ever to form part of the British Empire (see the *Survey for 1926*, Part III A, Section (xii) (*f*)).

total ' man power ' and material power of the human race. In any future war in which more than one Great Power was a belligerent, it was probable that there would be no neutrals and no non-combatants ; and in 1926 this appalling new fact was faced, and the logical action taken upon it, in the Act for the Organization of the Nation in Time of War which passed the French Chamber (with the approval of the Socialists as well as the parties of the Right) on the 7th March, 1927.

This sinister change in the world made it an imperative task of statesmanship to substitute some new system of international relations for the existing system of a Balance of Power between states which had not renounced the right to make war on one another— a mechanism which had been proved by more than four centuries of its operation on the arena of Europe to be hopelessly incapable of regulation by other means than resorting to war periodically. In the histories of other civilizations in which the institution of War had existed, this fatal defect in the machinery of the Balance of Power had usually generated a succession of wars in an ascending scale of violence until the Balance had ceased to deal devastation through ceasing to function at all. ' The outlawry of war ' had then been enforced by some Great Power which had fought on until no rival was left alive on the field ; and this had been the origin of the historic super-states : the Double Crown of Ancient Egypt ; the United Kingdom of Sumer and Akkad ; the ' Realm of the Lands ' which was founded by Cyrus the Persian ; the successive ascendancies of the Mauryas, the Guptas, and the Mughals which had preceded the British Raj in India ; the ' Middle Kingdom ' of the dynasties of T'sin and Han ; the Roman Empire ; the Caliphate of the Umayyads and 'Abbasids; the dominion of the Incas in the New World. All these super-states were guided, in their day, by a statesmanship which had beheld, if only fitfully, the vision of a universal and perpetual peace ; but their downfalls showed that none of them were able to escape the nemesis of their military origins. The violence which had been put forth in order to bring them into being had always fallen short of its aim by exhausting the material and spiritual energies of the particular civilization in which each super-state arose before the conqueror had succeeded in imposing his peace upon the whole of society. For this reason every super-state had broken down, and after each downfall Sisyphus had found himself at the foot of his mountain once again.

The problem with which Western Civilization was confronted by the inexorable threat of a war of annihilation was the problem of

working out some new international system which would effect the
' outlawry of war ' without demanding from the peoples of the world
the sacrifice of any vital element in the institution of self-government. The positive object of preserving full national self-government
was not less important than the negative object of outlawing war ;
for if the avoidance of annihilation was at stake in the one aspect
of the problem, the perpetuation of social vitality and creative power
was equally at stake in the other. In 1926 two great experiments
towards the solution of this world-problem were in progress. One
of them was the British Commonwealth, the other the international
League of Nations ; and so far from being mutually exclusive, these
two political organizations were so closely allied both in spirit and
in aim that a statesman who had taken an active part in the evolution of each could speak, in one sentence, of both of them.

> Shall we act in continuous friendly consultation in the true spirit of
> a Society of Nations [General Smuts asked his fellow Prime Ministers
> at the opening sitting of the Imperial Conference of 1921] or will there
> once more be a repetition of rival groups, of exclusive alliances, and
> finally of a terrible catastrophe more fatal than the one we have passed
> through ? That, to my mind, is the alternative. That is the parting
> of the ways at which we have arrived now.[1]

On the answers which that question was to receive in the Commonwealth and in the League the future of mankind depended.

(i) British Citizenship: Distinctions drawn between Different Categories of British Citizens by Foreign Governments.

(a) THE EXCLUSION, BY UNITED STATES LEGISLATION, OF BRITISH
SUBJECTS OF CERTAIN RACES AND PROVENANCES FROM IMMIGRA-
TION INTO THE UNITED STATES

The problem of Migration has been dealt with in the *Survey for
1924*,[2] and an account has there been given of the various legislative
measures enacted by the United States with the object of restricting
immigration as a whole and excluding entirely certain classes of
aliens. The main provisions under which certain British subjects
were forbidden to enter the United States as immigrants need therefore only be briefly summarized in this place. The United States
Immigration Act of the 5th February, 1917, prohibited the admission
into the country of immigrants, whether subjects of Great Britain
or of some other Power, who were natives of an ' Asiatic Barred Zone'
including India, Burma, Ceylon, and the Malay Peninsula, as well

---

[1] *Cmd.* 1474 of 1921, p. 25.   [2] Part I B.

as the islands of the East Indies.[1] The Act which came into force on the 3rd June, 1921, established the principle of admission of immigrants by quotas, but natives of the ' Barred Zone ' were expressly excluded from this system and the prohibition of their right of entry remained absolute. In the 1924 Act the clause regarding the ' Asiatic Barred Zone ' did not reappear, but the exclusion provisions were made more stringent than ever. The new Act prohibited the immigration into the United States of all aliens ' ineligible to citizenship ' ; and the interpretation given to this term by various decisions of the United States Supreme Court made it clear that, generally speaking, ' all aliens who are not White and of European origin or Black and of African Origin ' would thenceforward be excluded from the United States.[2]

(*b*) THE PRIVILEGED STATUS, UNDER THE UNITED STATES IMMIGRATION ACT OF 1924, OF BRITISH CITIZENS OF CANADIAN BIRTH

While the Government of the United States, by the successive acts of legislation mentioned above, were endeavouring to guard against any further influx into the country of aliens who, in their view, would form an undesirable element in the national composition (in which category were included natives of India and of other Oriental territories of the British Empire), they continued to accord specially favourable treatment to immigrants born in British North America—this being ' the stock which the United States most desired to attract '.[3]

Under the United States Immigration Act of 1921, aliens who had resided for one year in Canada or Newfoundland (and also in Mexico and the countries of Central and South America) were exempted from the application of the quota system. This provision enabled over 150,000 immigrants to enter the United States from Canada and Newfoundland during the ten months ending the 30th April, 1924 ; and the 1924 Act, which aimed at a drastic reduction in the total number of immigrants, accordingly confined the privilege of unrestricted immigration to persons born in Canada or Newfoundland or other countries adjacent to the United States, with their wives and unmarried children under the age of 18. Immigrants from Canada or Newfoundland not born in those countries were to be included in the quota of their country of origin.[4]

[1] *Op. cit.*, pp. 140–1.
[2] *Op. cit.*, pp. 147–8, citing an article by Mr. A. Warner Parker in *The American Journal of International Law*, January 1925.
[3] *Survey for 1924*, p. 106.
[4] *Op. cit.*, pp. 96–7.

(ii) **The Distinction between 'Passive' and 'Active' Belligerency: The 'Chanāq Incident' of September 1922.**

The theoretical distinction between 'passive' and 'active' belligerency of states members of the British Commonwealth, in the event of the British Empire being at war, has been explained in the Introduction.[1] On paper, this constitutional theory reconciled the unitary character of the Empire in regard to foreign states with the full autonomy and the complete equality of status of the states members of the Commonwealth in regard to one another. The practical crux of the situation was that a decision on the part of any state member of the Commonwealth, in the event of the Empire being at war, to refrain from translating its passive belligerency into active terms might have the appearance of being morally, even though not juridically, equivalent to a declaration of neutrality in a conflict in which one or more of the other states members were engaged ; and such a decision would therefore be apt to have unfortunate psychological consequences.

In such a situation the state member or states members which were committed to 'active' belligerency would probably be left with a certain feeling of resentment towards the sister community which had exercised its constitutional right not to enter into active co-operation in so vital a matter as any war must be ;[2] and although they might frankly admit the other party's right and might diplomatically conceal their own feelings, a more or less serious estrangement of feeling would be not unlikely to follow. On the other side, the unwillingness to allow such an estrangement to occur would reinforce the spontaneous loyalty and chivalry of the people of the 'passive' community towards the people of the sister communities to such an extent that, even if a majority of the electorate in the 'passive' community were opposed to 'active' belligerency, the Government of the 'passive' community could hardly perform its constitutional but invidious duty of taking the decision to abstain

---

[1] See pp. 1–3 above.

[2] The degree of such resentment would presumably vary in accordance with the gravity of the war in which the community that was committed to 'active' belligerency found itself engaged. Great Britain, for example, would not be likely to resent it if Canada contented herself with 'passive' belligerency in the event of Great Britain finding herself at war with Afghanistan. Resentment might arise, however, supposing that a 'local war' between Great Britain, or rather between Great Britain and India jointly, and Afghanistan were to grow in dimensions—for example, through intervention on the part of the U.S.S.R. It may be remarked that, in the Anglo-Afghan War of 1919, which was confined within local limits, it was never suggested that the self-governing Dominions overseas should take an active part.

from ' active ' belligerency without evoking protest and opposition at home from a strong minority—an opposition which it could only appease by overriding the will of the majority of the electorate and deciding, after all, to take an active part in the hypothetical war. In other words, the belligerency of the British Empire, though it might not implicate any state member of the British Commonwealth in active hostilities without its own consent, would almost certainly involve it in an estrangement of feeling from other states members and at the same time plunge it into a domestic controversy—two consequences which, in combination, might prove hardly less unfortunate than ' active ' belligerency itself and which nevertheless could not be averted by any constitutional safeguard, since they would arise not on the juridical but on the psychological plane.

This practical crux in the problem of British belligerency was illustrated during the Chanāq incident of September 1922—the only occasion between July 1914 and the close of the year 1926 on which any state member of the British Commonwealth found itself on the brink of active hostilities. In this instance hostilities were happily averted at the eleventh hour ; but the psychological effect of the situation upon the mutual relations of states members of the Commonwealth had time to declare itself nevertheless without ambiguity.

In recording this significant incident in the history of British Empire foreign relations, there is no need to recapitulate that long train of events in the international history of the Islamic World which, in September 1922, produced at Chanāq, on the Anatolian shore of the Dardanelles, an acute danger of armed conflict between the Government of Great Britain and the Government of the Turkish Great National Assembly of Angora.[1] It is sufficient to note, first, that if Great Britain and Turkey had resumed hostilities, the British Empire as a whole would have remained involved automatically in ' passive ' belligerency ; [2] and secondly that the crisis was a regional and not a world affair. While the destiny of the Black Sea Straits was a matter of profound importance for communities in Europe,

[1] For the histories of the abortive Peace Treaty of Sèvres and the definitive Peace Treaty of Lausanne between Turkey and the Allied Powers, see *H. P. C.*, vol. vi, Part II. The history of the Graeco-Turkish hostilities, which terminated in the autumn of 1922, is a postscript to the history of the General War of 1914–18, and therefore falls outside the scope of both the *H. P. C.* and the *Survey*.

[2] The whole British Empire was at that time still juridically at war with Turkey, since the state of war which had come into existence in 1914 had not yet been brought to an end by the exchange of ratifications of a peace treaty. Hostilities, however, had been suspended since the Mudros Armistice of the 30th October, 1918.

the Islamic World, and Russia, it did not affect directly the interests
of communities in those regions in which all the states members of
the British Commonwealth except the Irish Free State and Great
Britain herself happened to lie. Even if the situation at Chanāq in
September 1922 had resulted (as it happily did not result) in a
resumption of hostilities between Turkey and Great Britain, the
practical effect upon the national interests of the overseas states
members of the British Commonwealth would have been negligible.
This was so because hostilities between the British Empire and
Turkey would have been confined to the dimensions of a regional
war if they had been resumed at any time after the armistice concluded between Turkey and the Allies on the 30th October, 1918,
since that armistice had been one of the steps in the dissolution of
the Quadruple Alliance, and it was in virtue of that alliance that the
hostilities between Turkey and the British Empire during the years
1914 to 1918 had formed part of a General War in which the national
interests of all states members of the British Commonwealth had been
directly at stake. No doubt it was on this account that, from the
armistice of October 1918 onwards, His Majesty's Governments
overseas had been content to leave to His Majesty's Government in
Great Britain the whole responsibility for endeavouring to settle
accounts between the British Empire and Turkey. From October
1918 to September 1922 the Governments and the peoples of the
Overseas Dominions took it for granted that relations between
the British Empire and Turkey were no longer a matter of practical
interest to them. Hence the surprise created in the Dominions by
the action which was taken, on the 15th September, 1922, by the
Government of Great Britain.

At about 7 p.m. on that date,[1] that Government ' communicated '
by telegram ' with the Dominions, placing them in possession of the
facts and inviting them to be represented by contingents in the
defence of interests for which they have already made enormous
sacrifices and of soil which is hallowed by immortal memories of the
Anzacs '.[2] The receipt of this telegraphic communication created

[1] *The Times*, 18th September, 1922. According to a statement by Mr.
Mackenzie King in the House of Commons at Ottawa on the 1st February,
1923, the telegram was dispatched from London five minutes before midnight.

[2] Official statement on British policy in the Near East, issued by His
Majesty's Government in Great Britain, through Reuter's Agency, on the
16th September, 1922. The fact that the communication had been made by
telegram was not made public explicitly till a later date. The Canadian Prime
Minister, Mr. Mackenzie King, afterwards stated (in the House of Commons
at Ottawa on the 1st February, 1923), that ' the dispatch contained one
paragraph which I think may be regarded as the vital and essential one. It

uniform surprise in all the countries to whose Governments it was addressed,[1] though it did not evoke identic action on the part of those Governments themselves.

' Between 4.0 and 5.0 p.m.' on the afternoon of the 16th ' a reply was received at No. 10 Downing Street from Lord Jellicoe, Governor-General of New Zealand, stating that the Government of New Zealand associated themselves with the action proposed by the Allies and would be represented by a contingent '.[2] This decision was confirmed, on the 16th, by a full meeting of the New Zealand Cabinet, and was made public on the same day in a statement by the Prime Minister, Mr. Massey.[3]

The Australian Government decided, on or before the 17th, to notify Mr. Lloyd George that it desired to associate itself with His Majesty's Government in Great Britain in whatever action might be deemed necessary to ensure the freedom of the Straits and the sanctity of the Gallipoli Peninsula, and that it was prepared, if circumstances required it, to send a contingent of Australian troops. At the same time the Australian Prime Minister, Mr. Hughes, informed Mr. Lloyd George that the question would be brought before the Commonwealth Parliament on the 19th, in order that it might express its opinion on the whole matter.[4] In the course of the next few days the Commonwealth Government's reply to the communication of the 15th was made the subject of certain criticisms in Parliament, which Mr. Hughes sought to meet by explaining that the action which the Government at Westminster had asked the Australian Government to take was to join with the other Dominions and the Allies in maintaining the military *status quo* until a conference should be held.[5]

was to the effect that the British Government would be glad to know whether the Dominion Government wished to associate itself with the action which the British Government were taking and whether we would desire to be represented by a contingent '.

[1] ' This was the first and only intimation which the [Canadian] Government had received from the British Government of a situation in the Near East which had reached a critical stage and with respect of which there was reason to anticipate the necessity of making any kind of appeal for military assistance.'—Statement by Mr. Mackenzie King in the House of Commons at Ottawa, 1st February, 1923. On the same occasion, Mr. King stated that on the 16th September, 1922, before the official telegram from London had been received at the Prime Minister's Office at Ottawa from the Governor-General's Office, where it had to be decoded, the Canadian newspapers had already published a report of it which they had received from London by cable independently.   [2] *The Times*, 18th September, 1922.

[3] Text of this statement in *The Daily Telegraph*, 19th September, 1922.

[4] *The Times*, 18th September, 1922.

[5] *Ibid.*, 23rd September, 1922.

E

These responses from the South Sea Dominions, where popular sentiment was interested in the Dardanelles on account of the part played by the ' Anzac ' forces in the Dardanelles Expedition during the General War, were of a more positive character than the reactions which the communication of the 15th September, 1922, produced in South Africa and Canada.

The South African Government—whose reply was delayed for some days owing to the absence of General Smuts in a remote part of the country at the time when the telegram from London was received at Pretoria—expressed the opinion that the position had altered materially for the better and that there was no longer any call for the active intervention of the Union.[1]

The Canadian Prime Minister, Mr. Mackenzie King, and almost all the members of his Cabinet, were likewise absent from the capital of the Dominion when the telegram arrived at Ottawa, and they declined to make any public statements pending a special meeting of the Cabinet on the 18th,[2] though they telegraphed at once to His Majesty's Government in Great Britain to inquire whether they were at liberty to lay that Government's telegram before the Canadian Parliament—an inquiry to which the Government in Great Britain replied that the telegram was not suitable for publication textually.[3]   After a morning's sitting on the 18th, Mr. King announced that the communication from London did not contain sufficient information to provide the basis for a decision by the Canadian Government, and that they were therefore telegraphing for additional information.[4]   At the same time they asked the Government in Great Britain whether in their opinion it was desirable that the Canadian Parliament should be called to consider the matter, and received the reply that the Government of Great Britain saw no necessity for this.[5]   The line taken by the Canadian Government led to a public controversy between the Prime Minister and the leader of the opposition, Mr. Arthur Meighen.   The latter pointed out that, on the motion of the Prime Minister himself, the Canadian Parliament had specifically ratified the Peace Treaty of Sèvres, and argued from this that the Canadian Government ought to have responded to an appeal from His Majesty's Government in Great Britain to assist in preventing a violent overthrow of the

[1] The Daily Telegraph, 26th September, 1922.   The Union Government's reply was published on the 25th September.
[2] The Daily Telegraph, 18th September, 1922.
[3] Statement by Mr. Mackenzie King on the 1st February, 1923.
[4] The Daily Telegraph, 19th September, 1922.
[5] Statement by Mr. Mackenzie King on the 1st February, 1923.

Sèvres settlement. Mr. King replied that the Bill which he had introduced had been merely ' enabling ' legislation, and that Canada was not bound by the Sèvres Treaty, inasmuch as the treaty had never come into force owing to its repudiation by the Turks and its non-ratification by Great Britain.[1]

It was significant that the votes of states members of the British Commonwealth were divided on this issue in the Assembly of the League of Nations, which at that time happened to be holding its third session at Geneva.[2] On the 22nd September Dr. Nansen (Norway) moved a resolution in the Political Commission of the Assembly to request the Council ' to consider without delay what measures it might take with a view to the cessation of hostilities in Asia Minor, either by offering its good offices to the belligerents or in any other way '. This motion was vigorously seconded by Sir Joseph Cook (Australia), but was parried by Mr. H. A. L. Fisher (British Empire), with the support of Lord Robert Cecil (South Africa),[3] and Monsieur Hanotaux (France).

The danger of a resumption of hostilities ceased on the 29th September, 1922, when the Angora Government decided, on certain conditions, to accept the invitation from the three Principal Allied Powers to meet them in a conference.[4] Nevertheless, the incident produced a lasting psychological effect—especially, perhaps, in Canada—and this must be borne in mind in order to appreciate, not only the attitude subsequently taken up by Mr. Mackenzie King in regard to the ratification of the Peace Treaty of Lausanne,[5] but the general attitude of all the Dominion Governments and peoples towards the problem of British Empire foreign policy during the next few years. The gravity of the constitutional questions which the ' Chanāq Incident ' raised was brought out by Mr. Mackenzie King in a statement which he made in the House of Commons at

---

[1] *The Daily Telegraph*, 26th September, 1922 ; *The Times*, 27th September, 1922.

[2] It was also reported at the time in the London Press (e. g. in *The Times*, 23rd September, 1922, and *The Daily Telegraph*, 26th September, 1922) that a joint *démarche*, to suggest that the issue with Turkey should be referred to the League of Nations, was made to Mr. Lloyd George by the Dominion High Commissioners in London acting under instructions from their home Governments. This report appears to have been quite unfounded.

[3] On this occasion Lord Robert Cecil was presumably expressing his personal views rather than those of the Government which he was representing, since the South African Government was reported to have suggested, in its reply to the telegram of the 15th September, that the freedom of the Straits should be placed under the aegis of the League (*The Daily Telegraph*, 26th September, 1922).

[4] See *H. P. C.*, vol. iv, Part II.   [5] See Section (v) (b) below.

Ottawa on the 1st February, 1923. The Canadian Government, he stated, ' had repeatedly asked the British Government if they might be at liberty to bring down the correspondence. The British Government had in the most clear and emphatic way indicated its wish that the correspondence should not be laid before Parliament.'

> As regards the part [he concluded] which our Government has taken in this matter, I would say to my right hon. Friend (Mr. Meighen) that we have felt and feel very strongly that if the relations between the different parts of the British Empire are to be made of an enduring character, this will only be through a full recognition of the supremacy of Parliament, and this particularly with regard to matters which may involve participation in war. It is for Parliament to decide whether or not we should participate in wars in different parts of the world, and it is neither right nor proper for an individual, or for any group of individuals, to take any step which might limit the rights of Parliament in a matter which is of such great concern to all the people of our country.[1]

(iii) The Membership in the League of Nations of States Members of the British Commonwealth.

The separate membership in the League of first five, and then (after the admission of the Irish Free State) six, self-governing communities of the British Empire, was sometimes interpreted by foreign observers as a sign that the Empire was breaking up, and this impression was perhaps strengthened by the freedom with which each of these members took its own line when it did not happen to be in agreement with the policy of His Majesty's Government in Great Britain. A striking example of this independence of action was afforded by the discussion in the Assembly of the League on the 22nd September, 1922, which has been referred to above.[2] In reality, this freedom—taken for granted as it was by all states members of the British Commonwealth which were separately represented in the League—was a source of strength to the British Empire. If His Majesty's Government in Great Britain—not content with representing, in the League, the British Empire as such—had attempted to put pressure on the Governments of India and the Dominions in order to secure the uniform appearance of a united front at Geneva, then certainly the multiple representation of the

---

[1] It may be recalled that at this time the states members of the League of Nations had before them a draft amendment, proposed by Canada, to Article 10 of the Covenant, in which it was suggested that ' no member shall be under the obligation to engage in any act of war without the consent of its parliament, legislature, or other representative body ' (see p. 57 below).

[2] See p. 51 above.

Empire might have tended to produce a disruptive effect ; for the Dominions and India would undoubtedly have resented any attempt to restrict their rights as League members by private action behind the scenes. Since, however, the Dominions and India did not in fact find themselves exposed to any pressure of the kind on the part of His Majesty's Government in Great Britain, their delegates at Geneva felt no inhibition from maintaining close contact with their colleagues from Great Britain and consulting with them upon any questions of common interest that might arise, whether or not they eventually took identic action when the business in hand came before the Council or Assembly.

Thus, at Geneva, the several states members of the British Commonwealth were reminded of their unity in the midst of an alien though not unfriendly world of foreign states, whereas at the Imperial Conferences in London, at which only states members of the Commonwealth were represented, they were apt to be reminded more of their differences.

It may be added that the effect of the League in heightening the sense of unity among the states members of the Commonwealth seemed likely to be increased by the election of Canada to a seat on the League Council in 1927, since a situation which, until then, had only existed in the Assembly would now exist, as between two states members of the Commonwealth, on the Council as well.

(a) THE ADMISSION OF THE IRISH FREE STATE

The Irish Free State came into existence officially on the 6th December, 1922, one year after the date of signature of the Agreement with Great Britain. On the 20th April, 1923, Mr. Desmond FitzGerald, the Minister for External Affairs of the Free State, made formal application for admission to membership of the League of Nations, 'in accordance with the terms of Article 1 of the Covenant', and gave an undertaking that the Free State would ' accept the conditions laid down in Article 1 of the Covenant and . . . carry out all the obligations involved in Membership of the League '.[1] The Free State's application was placed on the agenda for the Fourth Assembly of the League, which opened on the 3rd September, 1923. The sub-committee of the Sixth Committee of the Assembly, to which this and other applications for admission were referred, based its investigations on the series of questions which were customarily

[1] Text of note in *League of Nations Monthly Summary*, vol. iii, No. 4, April 1923.

asked in connexion with the election of new members.[1] The second and third of these questions ran as follows :

(2). Is the Irish Free State recognized *de iure* or *de facto* and by what states ?

(3). Does the country possess a stable Government and well defined frontiers ?

In reply to the second question, the sub-committee noted ' that the Irish Free State is a Dominion forming part of the British Empire upon the same conditions as the other Dominions which are already Members of the League '. The third question they answered in the affirmative, adding that they ' had been informed that provision for the final delimitation of a part of the boundary [had] been made in the treaty, dated December 6th, 1922, embodied in the fundamental law constituting the Irish Free State '.

The sub-committee's report having been adopted by the Sixth Committee, the Free State was, on the 10th September, admitted to membership by the unanimous vote of the forty-six states represented in the Assembly.

(*b*) THE REGISTRATION AT GENEVA OF THE ARTICLES OF AGREEMENT OF THE 6TH DECEMBER, 1921, BY THE GOVERNMENT OF THE IRISH FREE STATE

On the 11th July, 1924, the representative of the Irish Free State at Geneva registered with the Secretariat of the League, in accordance with Article 18 of the Covenant,[2] the Agreement with Great Britain of the 6th December, 1921. His Majesty's Government in Great Britain was notified of this registration on the same day. On the 27th November a note was addressed by His Majesty's Government in Great Britain to the Secretary-General of the League raising objections to the action taken by the Irish Free State :

Since the Covenant of the League of Nations came into force, His Majesty's Government has consistently taken the view that neither it nor any conventions concluded under the auspices of the League are intended to govern relations *inter se* of various parts of the British Commonwealth. His Majesty's Government considers, therefore, that the terms of Article 18 of the Covenant are not applicable to the Articles of Agreement of December 6, 1921.

The Government of the Free State, however, maintained their

---

[1] For the form of this questionnaire see the *Survey for 1926*, Part I A, Section (i).

[2] ' Every treaty or international engagement entered into hereafter by any Member of the League shall be forthwith registered with the Secretariat and shall as soon as possible be published by it. No such treaty or international engagement shall be binding until so registered.'

point of view. In a statement [1] issued on the 15th December, Mr. Desmond FitzGerald, the Minister for External Affairs, pointed out that—

The Covenant of the League of Nations sets out the duties undertaken by every member of the League. There are no distinctions between the members—none has special privileges and none is exempt from the obligations set forth in the Covenant. Article 18 means that every treaty and international engagement entered into after January 1920 shall be registered. The Irish Free State as a member of the League, as well as every other member, is bound by this Article. As the treaty is the basis of the Free State's relations with the other members of the British Commonwealth of Nations, it was pre-eminently our duty to register. To have failed in this would have been to repudiate the Covenant, which can be done neither by the Free State nor by any other member of the League.

On the 18th December the Free State Government, in acknowledging receipt of a communication from the League Secretariat enclosing a copy of the British Government's letter of the 27th November, recapitulated their views in the following terms :

The Government of the Irish Free State cannot see that any useful purpose would be served by the initiation of a controversy as to the intention of any individual signatory to the Covenant. The obligations contained in Article 18 are, in their opinion, imposed in the most specific terms on every member of the League, and they are unable to accept the contention that the clear and unequivocal language of that article is susceptible of any interpretation compatible with the limitation which the British Government now seek to read into it. They accordingly dissent from the view expressed by the British Government that the terms of Article 18 are not applicable to the Treaty of December 6, 1921.

No further correspondence took place on the subject ; the agreement of the 6th December, 1921, like other agreements presented for registration with the League Secretariat, was published in the *League of Nations Treaty Series* (Volume XXVI), and in the next volume of the series there appeared the British note of the 27th November and the Free State Government's note of the 18th December.

The divergent views of the two parties in regard to this particular agreement were thus placed on record without any attempt being made to reconcile them. On the other hand, the underlying question of principle was afterwards dealt with in the Report of the Inter-Imperial Relations Committee which was adopted by the Imperial Conference of 1926. In the section of this report concerning procedure in relation to treaties, it was submitted that—

The making of the treaty in the name of the King as the symbol of

[1] *The Times*, 16th December, 1924.

the special relationship between the different parts of the Empire will render superfluous the inclusion of any provision that its terms must not be regarded as regulating *inter se* the rights and obligations of the territories on behalf of which it has been signed in the name of the King. In this connexion it must be borne in mind that the question was discussed at the Arms Traffic Conference in 1925, and that the Legal Committee of that Conference laid it down that the principle to which the foregoing sentence gives expression underlies all international conventions.

In the case of some international agreements the Governments of different parts of the Empire may be willing to apply between themselves some of the provisions as an administrative measure. In this case they should state the extent to which and the terms on which such provisions are to apply. Where international agreements are to be applied between different parts of the Empire, the form of a treaty between Heads of States should be avoided.

Since His Majesty's respective Governments in Great Britain and in the Irish Free State were authoritatively represented on the Inter-Imperial Relations Committee as well as in the Plenary Conference, it was to be presumed that the adoption, by the Conference, of the passage just quoted would preclude the recurrence of the controversy which had arisen over the registration of the agreement of the 6th December, 1921.

(c) The Action taken by Canada with a view to the Modification of Article 10 of the Covenant

During the First Assembly of the League in 1920 the Canadian delegation proposed the elimination from the text of the Covenant of Article 10, which ran as follows :

The members of the League undertake to respect and preserve as against external aggression the territorial integrity and existing political independence of all Members of the League. In case of any such aggression or in case of any threat or danger of such aggression the Council shall advise upon the means by which this obligation shall be fulfilled.

This and other suggested amendments to the Covenant were referred to a special committee appointed by the Council in March 1921 ; and this committee, after the Canadian proposal had also been considered by a commission of jurists, drew up, for submission to the Second Assembly, a resolution giving a detailed interpretation of Article 10. In the course of the discussions on the question which took place during the Second Assembly in September 1921, widely different opinions were expressed as to the legal bearing of Article 10 in relation to the other articles of the Covenant ; and in view of the difficulty of deciding between the legal and political arguments which were adduced both for and against the retention of the article in its original form, the Assembly did not vote on the proposed interpretative resolution, but decided to postpone consideration of the whole matter until the next Assembly.

At the Third Assembly in 1922, the Committee on Amendments to the Covenant found themselves unable to make any fresh recommendation, and the Canadian delegation, realizing that it would be impossible to secure the abrogation of Article 10, withdrew the proposal which had been made at the First Assembly, and suggested instead the following amendments :

(1) the addition at the end of Article 10 of the words ' taking into account the political and geographical circumstances of each state ' ;

(2) the addition of a new paragraph as follows : ' The opinion given by the Council in such cases shall be regarded as a matter of the highest importance, and shall be taken into consideration by all the Members of the League, who shall use their utmost endeavours to conform to the conclusions of the Council; but no Member shall be under the obligation to engage in any act of war without the consent of its parliament, legislature, or other representative body.'

The Assembly felt that it would be desirable for states members to be given the opportunity of considering these proposals in detail before they were discussed, and therefore postponed consideration of them for another year. During the interval between the Third and Fourth Assemblies, the Canadian amendments were circulated to states members, twenty-five of whom had communicated their views to the Secretariat by September 1923. Only four of the replies received [1] conveyed unqualified approval of the Canadian proposals ; the majority of the states who answered raised objections to one or both of the amendments, or considered that the question should be left open until some decision had been reached with regard to a Treaty of Mutual Guarantee.

On the basis of the opinions received, the First Committee of the Fourth Assembly drew up the following resolution interpreting Article 10 of the Covenant ' so far as regards the points raised by the Canadian delegation '.

It is in conformity with the spirit of Article 10 that, in the event of the Council considering it to be its duty to recommend the application of military measures in consequence of an aggression or danger or threat of an aggression, the Council shall be bound to take account, more particularly, of the geographical situation and of the special conditions of each state.

[1] Those from Austria, Bulgaria, Hungary, and Uruguay. The texts of all the letters received are printed as annexes to the Minutes of the First Committee of the Fourth Assembly (*Records of the Fourth Assembly*, Geneva, 1923).

It is for the constitutional authorities of each Member to decide, in reference to the obligation of preserving the independence and the integrity of the territory of Members, in what degree the Member is bound to assure the execution of this obligation by employment of its military forces.

The recommendation made by the Council shall be regarded as being of the highest importance, and shall be taken into consideration by all the Members of the League with the desire to execute their engagements in good faith.

In the view of Monsieur Rolin, who acted as Rapporteur for the First Committee, this resolution would not alter the sense of Article 10, but would merely clarify it, and would make the legal status of the Council's recommendation clear and unequivocal. When the resolution was put to the vote in the Assembly, however, one state (Persia) voted against it and twenty-two of the states represented at the Assembly were absent or abstained from voting. Since a resolution containing an interpretation of the Covenant could only be approved by a unanimous vote of the Assembly, the resolution was declared not to have been adopted.

Thereafter the Canadian Government seem to have abandoned their object of securing the amendment of Article 10. At the Fifth Assembly of 1924, during the discussion of the Protocol for the Pacific Settlement of International Disputes, the Canadian delegate, Senator Dandurand, expressed the hope ' that it will be possible to find, in the Protocol . . . the policy expressed in last year's resolution interpreting Article 10 '. Judging from the attitude subsequently adopted by Canada towards the Geneva Protocol,[1] it would appear that this hope was not fulfilled.

(d) The Candidature of the Irish Free State (1926) and the Election of Canada (1927) to a Temporary Seat on the League Council

During the Seventh Assembly of the League in 1926 a British Dominion, the Irish Free State, made known its desire to be elected to a non-permanent seat on the Council. The principal delegate of the Irish Free State, Mr. Desmond Fitzgerald, Minister for External Affairs, appears to have decided on this course on his own authority without consultation with Dublin.[2] The general attitude of the British Empire representatives at the Assembly made it clear that the Free State had little chance of securing one of the nine temporary

[1] See *Survey for 1925*, Vol. II, pp. 3, 5, and 6.
[2] See *The Times*, 17th September, 1926.

seats to which elections had to be made during this session ; [1] and when the voting took place on the 16th September, the Free State came thirteenth on the list, having received ten votes. Only eight states obtained the necessary absolute majority of twenty-five votes on the first count, and a second ballot was therefore taken, in which the Free State received four votes.

On the previous day, the 15th September, the principal delegate of Canada, Sir George Foster, had drawn the attention of the Assembly to the peculiar position of the British Commonwealth in connexion with representation on the Council.

> We have heard much [he said] of the claims for representation on the Council of cultural and racial groups, but we have not, during the six years that the League of Nations has been in operation, heard anything of that group, if I may call it such, of Members of the League of Nations made up of the overseas dominions and possessions of the British Empire. . . . These different dominions for seven years, more or less, have been units of the League of Nations and Members of this Assembly, occupying a position of absolute equality with every other nation Member of the League. . . . During those six years you have never heard, with one exception (because I understand this morning that the delegates of the Irish Free State propose to submit a claim for a seat on the Council) of any demand or claim from that group of free peoples for special precedence or consideration or for a place in the Council. . . . So far as my country and the other members of the British overseas countries are concerned, we have not hitherto made and are not now making any claim for a seat on the Council of the League. But . . . we consider that we have equal rights to representation on the Council and otherwise with every one of the fifty-six Members of the League of Nations, and . . . we do not propose to waive that right.

Although Canada thus refrained, in 1926, from soliciting election, in the voting on the 16th September she received two votes and so found herself sharing with Denmark, Estonia, and Siam the bottom place on the list of eighteen states for which votes had been cast.

A year later, during the Eighth Assembly of 1927, Canada sought election and was not disappointed. In coming forward as one of the six candidates for the three vacant seats, Canada offered herself, on this occasion, both as a member of the British Empire and as a representative of the American continent. Since the basis of representation in the Council was to some extent geographical, this latter claim carried weight—especially since the disappearance of Brazil had diminished the number of possible candidates from South America. There was, however, another American candidate, Cuba, and it was inevitable that she and Canada should appear in the light of alterna-

---

[1] See the *Survey for 1926*, Part I A, Section (i).

tive candidates. Thus, while it was known that Canada would have the support of all the British delegations, her election was dependent on the votes of the South American states, and until the voting actually took place on the 15th September, Cuba was generally considered to have a better chance of election than Canada.[1] In the event, both states received non-permanent seats, Cuba by forty votes and Canada by twenty-six (the absolute majority required being twenty-five).[2]

It was rumoured that the Canadian Cabinet had not been of one mind in regard to the candidature for a seat on the Council, but that the French-Canadian members of the Government had carried the day.[3] The news of Canada's success was received in the country at large with a lack of comment which was surprising, in view of the fact that the Government had sought and accepted a seat on the Council without consulting either Parliament or people and had thus taken a step which would be bound to involve the country, to a certain extent, in international affairs from which it had hitherto held aloof. This departure from traditional policy was indeed criticized in some quarters, but on the whole the election seems to have been welcomed, as setting the final seal on Canada's autonomous nationhood.[4]

(e) The Exercise of League Mandates by South Africa, Australia, and New Zealand, as well as by the British Empire

On the 7th May, 1919, the Supreme Council, meeting in Paris, decided on the allocation of the mandates over ex-German possessions in Africa and the Pacific. In selecting the mandatories the rule was followed, generally speaking, that the country whose own territories were nearest to the territory in question should be made responsible for it ; and where that country was a member of the British Empire the mandate was allocated, with one exception, to

---

[1] See The Times, 15th September, 1927.

[2] Some of these votes may have been won for Canada by Mr. Dandurand's speech in the Assembly on the 12th September, 1927, in which he emphasized the interest taken by the French Canadians in the problem of minorities and intimated that the Canadian Government did not share the views of His Majesty's Government in Great Britain in regard to arbitration and to the optional clause of the statute of the Permanent Court. Canada may also have benefited from the elimination of the Belgian candidature at the morning sitting on the day on which the election took place in the afternoon. This was quite unexpected and left many delegations with a vote to spare which could fall to either Canada, Greece, or Portugal.

[3] See The Manchester Guardian, 1st October, 1927.

[4] See The Manchester Guardian, loc. cit.

the particular Dominion concerned and not to the British Empire as a whole. Thus the Union of South Africa received the mandate for South-West Africa, Australia that for New Guinea, and New Zealand that for Samoa. In the case of Nauru Island, however, the British Empire was constituted the mandatory; and by an agreement of the 2nd July, 1919, Great Britain, Australia, and New Zealand arranged for the administration of the island and the exploitation of the phosphates which made it valuable on terms which provided for the appointment of an administrator for the first five years by Australia, and thereafter in a manner to be agreed on by the three Governments.

All the mandates above mentioned belonged to the ' C ' class, agreed drafts for which were received by the Secretariat of the League of Nations on the 9th December, 1920, and which were brought into operation, on receiving the approval of the League Council, on the 17th December, 1920.[1]

(iv) **The Diplomatic and Consular Representation of States Members of the British Commonwealth (other than Great Britain) and of Foreign States in one another's Capitals.**

(a) The U.S.-Canadian International Joint Commission

On the 7th August, 1927, three days after the Three-Power Naval Conference at Geneva had ended in failure, the peoples of Canada and the United States found occasion to celebrate the peaceful and friendly relations which had long subsisted between them at the opening of a Peace Bridge across the Niagara River. The speeches delivered, at the inaugural ceremony at Buffalo, by the Prince of Wales, the Vice-President of the United States, the Prime Minister of Canada, and the Prime Minister of Great Britain gave expression to the common pride which the peoples of Canada and of the United States took in the peace and goodwill which had long reigned from end to end of the 3,898 miles of their common frontier.

Such pride was well justified, since this happy state of affairs could not have been established without wisely directed and steadily sustained efforts on both sides. For 1,525 out of the total 3,898 miles the U.S.-Canadian frontier followed artificial lines which ignored, and indeed conflicted with, the physical configuration of the North

[1] See *H. P. C.*, vol. vi, Ch. VI, Part IV. For the administration of the mandate for South-West Africa, see the *Survey for 1920–3*, Part V, Section (iv); and for the administration of the Pacific Mandates see the *Survey for 1926*, Part III B, Section (iii).

American continent ; and the waterways which constituted the rest of the boundary provided a ' natural frontier ' only in theory, since, with every fresh advance in technique, these lakes and rivers became the media of a more and more intimate contact between the countries on their opposite shores.[1] The increasing utilization of these common waters for domestic and sanitary purposes, for navigation, for irrigation, and for the generation of power created a correspondingly greater frequency of occasions for international controversy.   Other sections of the frontier—particularly at the two extremities, between the Atlantic and the St. Lawrence and again between the Rocky Mountains and the Pacific—had actually been the subjects of long controversies in the past, and, earlier still, the populations on either side of the frontier had been alienated from one another not only by diplomatic disagreements but by wars. The duel between the French-Canadians and the New Englanders had occupied the first three-quarters of the eighteenth century ; and the struggle between Republicans and Loyalists in the Thirteen Colonies during the Revolutionary War had been resumed on the border between New York State and Ontario during the War of 1812. Thus the subsequent demilitarization of the frontier was no mean achievement. Moreover, for the maintenance of good relations, the existence of friendly feelings was not enough. The increasing complexity of the trans-frontier economic relations in the border-zone called for perpetual adjustment, and provision for this need was made in a treaty, signed at Washington on the 11th January, 1909, between the United Kingdom and the United States relating to boundary waters and questions arising along the boundary between Canada and the United States.[2] This treaty dealt with the problem in a manner which took into account the then already accomplished fact of Canada's full nationhood, by setting up a standing body entitled the International Joint Commission on which not the United Kingdom but the Dominion of Canada and the United States were represented on an equal footing.

The Commission thus established consisted [3] of six members, three of whom were appointed by the President of the United States and

[1] See the British Parliamentary Paper *Cmd.* 2510 of 1925 for the text of a treaty between Canada and the United States of America to define more accurately and to complete the international boundary between the two countries. This treaty was signed at Washington on the 24th February, 1925, and ratifications were exchanged at the same place on the 17th July of the same year.

[2] Text in *Cmd.* 5223 of 1910.

[3] See *The Canada Year Book*, 1926, published by authority of the Canadian Minister of Trade and Commerce, pp. 971–2.

three by His Britannic Majesty on the recommendation of the Government of Canada. The members did not act by national sections but as a single international body. There was a Canadian Chairman and an American Chairman, who presided over the Commission alternately at meetings held on their respective sides of the frontier. There were likewise two secretaries, one in charge of the Commission's offices at Ottawa and the other of those in Washington. The Commission held two fixed meetings every year—one in Washington on the first Tuesday in April and the other at Ottawa on the first Tuesday in October—while other meetings or public hearings were held at such times and places as the two chairman might determine.

By the treaty (Art. 8) the Commission was given jurisdiction over, and was empowered to pass upon, all cases involving the use or obstruction or diversion of certain waters with respect to which, under Articles 3 and 4 of the treaty, the approval of the Commission was required. In this matter, the Commission was to render its decision by a majority vote, while, in the event of an equal division of votes, the two Governments were to endeavour to adjust the difference by direct negotiation. Frontier controversies falling outside the scope of Articles 3 and 4 might be referred to the Commission, by either one of the two Governments, for examination and report (Art. 9), though the consequent reports of the Commission were not to be regarded as decisions of the questions or matters so submitted, either on the facts or on the law, and were in no way to have the character of an arbitral award. By the common consent of the two Governments, however, controversies falling within the scope of Article 9 might also be referred to the Commission for decision (in this case likewise by a majority vote). In such a case, if the Commission were equally divided or were otherwise unable to render a decision, the matter was to be referred to an umpire chosen in accordance with the procedure prescribed in the fourth, fifth, and sixth paragraphs of Article 45 of the Hague Convention of the 18th October, 1907, for the Pacific Settlement of International Disputes, and such umpire was to have power to render a final decision (Art. 10).

The Treaty of Washington was brought into force by exchange of ratifications on the 5th May, 1910, and between that date and the end of the year 1926 the Commission had disposed of a large number of cases under Articles 3 and 4 and had also carried out several investigations under Article 9.[1] Some of these matters were only of

[1] The information in this paragraph is taken from The Canada Year Book, 1926, loc. cit.

minor importance, but others involved great natural resources and large capital investments on both sides of the frontier and affected the health and prosperity of millions of people. To this class belonged the power cases at Sault Sainte Marie, the settlement of which involved the levels of Lake Superior and the material interests of cities on its shores ; the Pollution of Boundary Waters Investigation ; the St. Lawrence Navigation and Power Investigation ; the Lake of the Woods Investigation ;[1] and several others. On the other hand, no questions had as yet been brought before the Commission under the terms of Article 10. Under Article 6 the Commission had also been charged with the measurement, and the division for irrigation purposes, of the waters of the St. Mary and Milk Rivers in Alberta and Montana. Owing to certain ambiguities in the text of the treaty, difficulties were found in arriving at a satisfactory settlement of this problem ; but eventually the Commission worked out a practicable compromise, which proved generally acceptable, by bringing together on the spot the parties directly interested.[2]

The treaty on which the existence of the International Joint Commission depended was terminable, after a first currency of five years, by the presentation of twelve months' notice in writing by either party, but in 1926 there seemed every likelihood that an arrangement which had worked so well for sixteen years would be maintained in perpetuity.[3]

(b) The Diplomatic Representation of Canada in Washington and of the United States at Ottawa

The establishment, under the treaty concluded on the 11th January, 1909, between the United Kingdom and the United States, of a standing U.S.-Canadian diplomatic body in the shape of the Joint International Commission,[4] and the temporary presence in Washington, at the latter end of the General War of 1914–18, of a Canadian War Mission which virtually performed the functions of a diplomatic legation, were two events which prepared the way for the

[1] The Commission submitted its final report on the results of this investigation on the 18th May, 1917. Its recommendations formed the basis of a convention between the United States and Canada to regulate the level of the Lake of the Woods which was signed at Washington on the 24th February, 1925 (Text in British Parliamentary Paper, *Cmd.* 2511 of 1925).

[2] In April 1928 there were indications that the question of the St. Mary and Milk Rivers was likely to be reopened (See *The Times*, 10th April, 1928).

[3] Certain questions which arose between Canada and the United States concerning the control of waters and other frontier problems during the years 1925–7 are dealt with in an appendix to the present volume.

[4] For the functions of this body see Section (iv) (a) above.

direct reciprocal diplomatic representation of the two countries in one another's capitals on a permanent footing in the manner customary in the relations between sovereign independent states. This consummation—which was simply the corollary, in the diplomatic sphere, of the accomplished fact of Canada's attainment of full nationhood—took place between the termination of the War and the end of the year 1926.

'At London and in Paris during 1918 and 1919 the Canadian Prime Minister had discussed with the British Prime Minister, as well as with the Foreign and Colonial Secretary, the importance and desirability of direct diplomatic representation of Canada at Washington. The subject was surrounded with certain difficulties of international import, and there was a possible danger that such a step might be taken to imply a lessening of the ties which connected Canada with Great Britain and her sister nations. Apprehension on this subject was eventually removed, and finally an arrangement was reached in May 1920 which was announced to the Canadian Parliament in the following terms : [1]

As a result of recent discussions an arrangement has been concluded between the British and Canadian Governments to provide more complete representation at Washington of Canadian interests than hitherto existed. Accordingly, it has been agreed that His Majesty, on advice of his Canadian Ministers, shall appoint a Minister Plenipotentiary who will have charge of Canadian affairs and will at all times be the ordinary channel of communication with the United States Government in matters of purely Canadian concern, acting upon instructions from, and reporting direct to, the Canadian Government. In the absence of the Ambassador, the Canadian Minister will take charge of the whole embassy and of the representation of Imperial as well as Canadian interests. He will be accredited by His Majesty to the President with the necessary powers for the purpose.

This new arrangement will not denote any departure either on the part of the British Government or of the Canadian Government from the principle of the diplomatic unity of the British Empire.

The need for this important step has been fully realized by both Governments for some time. For a good many years there has been direct communication between Washington and Ottawa, but the constantly increasing importance of Canadian interests in the United States has made it apparent that Canada should be represented there in some distinctive manner, for this would doubtless tend to expedite negotiations, and naturally first-hand acquaintance with Canadian conditions would promote good understanding. In view of the peculiarly close relations that have always existed between the people of Canada and those of the

---

[1] A corresponding announcement, partly in identical terms, was made in the House of Commons at Westminster by Mr. Bonar Law on the 11th May, 1920 (*The Times*, 21st May, 1924).

United States, it is confidently expected as well that this new step will have the very desirable result of maintaining and strengthening the friendly relations and co-operation between the British Empire and the United States.

' Debates in the Canadian Parliament followed, the most important taking place on the 21st April, 1921. In support of the proposal it was pointed out, *inter alia*, that for many years Canadian Ministers, acting virtually as diplomatic representatives, had been in the habit of conferring and negotiating with the American Government. If such temporary representation was sound in principle, as well as advantageous, there could be no serious objection to permanent diplomatic representation. Moreover, the principle was actually in operation, as the members of the Canadian section of the International Joint Commission were appointed by the Crown on the recommendation of the Canadian Government.' [1]

Nevertheless, the Canadian Government, now that its title to accredit a separate diplomatic representative to the President of the United States had received this public recognition, did not proceed forthwith to make an appointment ; and the right thus secured by Canada was actually first exercised—in virtue of the most-favoured-Dominion-status clause in the Anglo-Irish Agreement of the 6th December, 1921—by the Irish Free State, whose first Minister at Washington, Professor Timothy Smiddy, presented his credentials to President Coolidge on the 7th October, 1924.[2] It was not till the 7th June, 1926, that the offer of the post of Canadian diplomatic representative in Washington to Mr. Vincent Massey was announced unofficially.[3] On the 10th November an Order in Council was passed appointing Mr. Massey Envoy Extraordinary and Minister Plenipotentiary of His Britannic Majesty in Washington to represent the interests of the Dominion of Canada.[4] Mr. Massey presented his credentials on the 18th February, 1927.[5]

On the 3rd February, 1927, Mr. William Phillips was appointed United States Minister to Canada.[6] Mr. Phillips presented his credentials on the 1st June, 1927.[7]

---

[1] Sir Robert Borden in *The Yale Review*, July 1923. It may be noted that, in the original plan, it appears to have been contemplated that the Canadian Minister in Washington should take charge of the British Embassy in the absence of the Ambassador ; but this part of the plan appears to have been abandoned subsequently.   [2] *The Times*, 9th October, 1924.

[3] *Ibid.*, 24th September and 26th November, 1926.

[4] *Ibid.*, 13th and 26th November, 1926.

[5] *The United States Daily*, 19th February, 1927.

[6] *Ibid.*, 4th February, 1927.

[7] *Ibid.*, and *The Times*, 2nd June, 1927.

In the year 1928 the Canadian Government proceeded to arrange with the French and Japanese Governments for reciprocal diplomatic representation. On the 10th January, 1928, the Canadian Prime Minister, Mr. Mackenzie King, announced that his Government had decided to establish a Legation in Paris, in order to extend the scope of the work hitherto carried on by the Canadian Commissioner-General in France, and that the French Government held a corresponding view as to the establishment of a French Legation in Canada. The Canadian Parliament would therefore be asked to make provision for the establishment of a Canadian Legation in Paris at an early date.[1] The necessary legislation does not appear to have been introduced into the House of Commons at Ottawa up to the time of writing, but a Bill authorizing the establishment of a French Legation in Canada passed the French Chamber, without discussion, on the 16th March, 1928.[2]

The official announcement that an exchange of Ministers had also been arranged with Japan was made by the Governor-General in the speech from the Throne at the opening of Parliament on the 26th January, 1928. Canada had hitherto been represented in Japan by a Trade Commissioner and Japan in Canada by a Consul-General, but the Canadian Government seems to have felt that a more formal method of representation would be desirable, in view of the growing importance of Canada's commercial and other relations with the Far East.[3] The Government's decision, however, was criticized by the Opposition, on the ground that the policy of replacing Trade Commissioners in foreign countries by Ministers was likely to lead to dangerous complications. In a debate in the House of Commons at Ottawa on the 21st January, 1928, the Leader of the Conservative Opposition, Mr. Bennett, expressed the opinion that the appointment of a Minister at Tokyo would be a particularly dangerous experiment, since Canada might thereby become involved in controversies over immigration and other matters.[4]

(c) THE DIPLOMATIC REPRESENTATION OF THE IRISH FREE STATE
IN WASHINGTON

The following provisions were contained in the Anglo-Irish Agreement of the 6th December, 1921, Articles 1 and 2 :

1. Ireland shall have the same constitutional status in the Community of Nations known as the British Empire as the Dominion of Canada, the

---

[1] *The Times*, 11th January, 1928.   [2] *Ibid.*, 17th March, 1928.
[3] See *The Manchester Guardian*, 27th January, 1928.
[4] See *The Times*, 1st February, 1928.

Commonwealth of Australia, the Dominion of New Zealand, and the Union of South Africa, with a Parliament having powers to make laws for the peace, order and good government of Ireland and an Executive responsible to that Parliament, and shall be styled and known as the Irish Free State.

2. Subject to the provisions hereinafter set out the position of the Irish Free State in relation to the Imperial Parliament and Government and otherwise shall be that of the Dominion of Canada, and the law, practice and constitutional usage governing the relationship of the Crown or the representative of the Crown and of the Imperial Parliament to the Dominion of Canada shall govern their relationship to the Irish Free State.

By the date of signature of the agreement containing this provision, one of the recognized elements of Dominion Status on the Canadian pattern (in virtue of the announcements made in the Parliaments at Westminster and Ottawa in May 1920 [1]) was the right to accredit a separate diplomatic representative to the President of the United States. The Government of the Irish Free State having intimated its desire to exercise this right, the following correspondence,[2] respecting the appointment of an Irish Free State Minister Plenipotentiary at Washington, was exchanged between the Governments of His Britannic Majesty and of the United States:

Sir Esmé Howard to the Secretary of State of the United States.

British Embassy, Washington,
June 24, 1924.

Sir,—Under instructions from His Majesty's Principal Secretary of State for Foreign Affairs, I have the honour to inform you that His Majesty's Government have come to the conclusion that it is desirable that the handling of matters at Washington exclusively relating to the Irish Free State should be confided to a Minister Plenipotentiary accredited to the United States Government. Such a Minister would be accredited by His Majesty the King to the President of the United States and he would be furnished with credentials which would enable him to take charge of all affairs relating only to the Irish Free State. He would be the ordinary channel of communication with the United States Government on these matters.

Matters which are of Imperial concern or which affect other Dominions in the Commonwealth in common with the Irish Free State will continue to be handled as heretofore by this Embassy.

The arrangements proposed by His Majesty's Government would not denote any departure from the principle of the diplomatic unity of the Empire. The Irish Minister would be at all times in the closest touch with His Majesty's Ambassador, and any question which may arise as to whether a matter comes within the category of those to be handled

[1] See Section (iv) (*b*) above.
[2] Text reprinted from British Parliamentary Paper *Cmd.* 2202 of 1924.

by the Irish Minister or not would be settled by consultation between them.   In matters falling within his sphere the Irish Minister would not be subject to the control of His Majesty's Ambassador, nor would His Majesty's Ambassador be responsible for the Irish Minister's actions.

In communicating to you these proposals, which His Majesty's Government trust will promote the maintenance and development of cordial relations between the British Empire and the United States, I have been instructed to express the hope that the United States Government will concur in the appointment of an Irish Free State Minister at Washington on the footing I have indicated above.   As regards questions such as the precedence to be attributed to the Irish Minister or any other points which the United States Government may desire to raise in connexion with the appointment, His Majesty's Government will await the views of the United States Government.

The Secretary of State of the United States to Sir Esmé Howard.

Department of State, Washington,
June 28, 1924.

Excellency,—I have the honour to acknowledge the receipt of your note of June 24, 1924, by which, under instructions from His Majesty's Principal Secretary of State for Foreign Affairs, you inform me of the conclusion which His Majesty's Government has reached that it is desirable that the handling of matters at Washington exclusively relating to the Irish Free State should be confided to a Minister Plenipotentiary accredited by His Majesty the King with credentials which would enable him to take charge of all affairs relating only to the Irish Free State.

Responding to the hope which you express on behalf of your Government that the Government of the United States will concur in the appointment of an Irish Free State Minister at Washington in conformity with the proposals of His Majesty's Government as set out in your note, I have the honour and the pleasure to inform you that the President, always happy to meet the wish of His Majesty's Government in every proper way, will be pleased to receive a duly accredited Minister Plenipotentiary of the Irish Free State on the footing you indicate.

The first holder of this new diplomatic post, Professor Timothy Smiddy, presented his credentials to President Coolidge on the 7th October, 1924.[1]   The first United States Minister to the Irish Free State, Mr. F. A. Sterling, was appointed on the 3rd February, 1927 (simultaneously with the first United States Minister to Canada),[2] and presented his credentials at Dublin on the 27th July, 1927.[3]

In thus exercising their right under the agreement of 1921, the Government of the Irish Free State were no doubt actuated in part

[1] *The Times*, 9th October, 1924.
[2] *The United States Daily*, 5th February, 1927.
[3] *The Times*, 28th July, 1927.

by a wish to demonstrate—both to their own countrymen and to the world at large—the reality of that full self-government which the agreement had assured to this newly created state member of the British Commonwealth. The demonstration of that fact to the people of the United States was, of course, as desirable in the interests of Great Britain as in those of the Free State itself. At the same time, the Irish Free State had a special relation to the United States which was as intimate, in its way, as that of Canada. While Canada was bound to the United States by geographical ties—the bipartite ownership and occupation of the entire North American Continent north of the Rio Grande, and the joint user of waterways and water power on a common frontier 3,898 miles long—the Irish Free State was bound to the United States by a tie of kinship. In 1927 it was officially reckoned by the United States Government that the element in the existing population of the United States which had been contributed by immigration from the territory since comprised in the Irish Free State amounted to no less than 9,769,070 persons— that is, to about 8 per cent. of the existing population of the United States and to more than three times the existing population of the Free State itself. Since these Irish-Americans had notoriously exercised an important effect not only upon the relations between the United States and the British Empire but upon those between Great Britain and Ireland, it was evidently desirable for the Irish Free State to enter into direct diplomatic relations with a country whose citizen-body included this great Irish community overseas.[1]

Thus it was not an accident that Canada was the first state member of the British Commonwealth, other than Great Britain, to secure the right of separate diplomatic representation in Washington, and the Irish Free State the first member to exercise it. The other states members of the Commonwealth had not yet followed the Canadian and Irish precedent by the end of the year 1926. It is true that on the 2nd December, 1926, the following announcement was made, in a speech addressed to the New York Chamber of Commerce, by the Australian Trade Commissioner, Sir Hugh Denison (apparently with reference to the recently published report of the Inter-Imperial

---

[1] All the Irish residents in the United States had not, of course, exchanged their British citizenship for American citizenship ; and indeed persons hailing from the Irish Free State must have accounted for a high proportion of the British subjects resident in the United States at this time. The British consuls in the United States, however, in dealing with the affairs of this category of British subjects, appear to have continued, even after the accrediting of an Irish Minister to the President, to be responsible to the British Ambassador.

Relations Committee of the Imperial Conference which had been just sitting in London) : [1]

The new agreement accords Australia, as it does other countries in the British Empire, the right to treat with America as a self-governing nation ; the same diplomatic relations that rule between America and other countries probably, in the not far distant future, will exist between my country and yours.[2]

There was no indication, however, that any decision, on the lines suggested by this announcement, had been taken, or indeed was being contemplated by, the Australian Government at that time; and rather more than a year later the Commonwealth Prime Minister, Mr. Bruce, was reported[3] to have declared explicitly that Australia did not contemplate following, in this matter, the Canadian precedent.

(d) THE ISSUE OF EXEQUATURS TO FOREIGN CONSULS IN THE DOMINIONS

This matter was dealt with in the following passage of the report of the Inter-Imperial Relations Committee of the Imperial Conference of 1926—a report which was unanimously adopted by the Conference on the 19th November of that year.

A question was raised with regard to the practice regarding the issue of exequaturs to Consuls in the Dominions. The general practice hitherto, in the case of all appointments of Consuls de Carrière in any part of the British Empire, has been that the foreign Government concerned notifies His Majesty's Government in Great Britain, through the diplomatic channel, of the proposed appointment and that, provided that it is clear that the person concerned is, in fact, a Consul de Carrière, steps have been taken, without further formality, for the issue of His Majesty's exequatur. In the case of consuls other than those de Carrière, it has been customary for some time past to consult the Dominion Government concerned before the issue of the exequatur.

The Secretary of State for Foreign Affairs informed us that His Majesty's Government in Great Britain accepted the suggestion that in future any application by a foreign Government for the issue of an exequatur to any person who was to act as Consul in a Dominion should be referred to the Dominion Government concerned for consideration and that, if the Dominion Government agreed to the issue of the exequatur, it would be sent to them for counter-signature by a Dominion Minister. Instructions to this effect had indeed already been given.

[1] See *Cmd.* 2768 of 1926, pp. 26–7.
[2] *The Times*, 4th and 6th December, 1926.
[3] *Ibid.*, 16th January, 1928.

(v) Co-operation between States Members of the Commonwealth in the Conduct of Foreign Relations.

(a) THE PERSONAL CONTACT BETWEEN PRIME MINISTERS IN THE IMPERIAL CONFERENCES OF 1921, 1923, and 1926, AND THE SUPPLEMENTATION OF THIS BY OTHER METHODS OF COMMUNICATION AND CONSULTATION.

Before the close of the General War of 1914–18 it had come to be recognized by all concerned, as an axiom of Imperial statesmanship about which there could be no dispute, that the sole completely satisfactory method of communication and consultation between states members of the British Commonwealth in regard to British Empire foreign policy was to be found in personal contact between Prime Ministers.

During the last years of the War and the first months of the Peace Conference of Paris, when in every self-governing community in the Empire the Prime Ministers were in large measure released from the ordinary cares of party politics by the paramount duty of attending to the executive conduct of vital affairs in which there was no fundamental difference of aim either between the different parties in each community or between the several communities themselves, the ideal of continuous personal contact between Prime Ministers was substantially realized. ' In 1917 the Dominion Prime Ministers came to London, and with the four members of the British War Cabinet sat as an Imperial War Cabinet to examine the war situation and agree upon what further common measures could be taken to assure victory. In 1918 they came again. Only this time there was a subtle change in their attitude. They came not for information alone but as of right, to discharge their responsibility to their own peoples for seeing that the War was properly conducted. During 1918 the Imperial War Cabinet, instead of being an *ad hoc* body for the exchange of information and ideas, sat alternatively with the British War Cabinet, and became, in fact, the plenary authority which dealt with the major problems of the War. It was the same at the Peace Conference. The British Empire delegation consisted of three British delegates, the Dominion Ministers, and a representative of India. Every major problem of the Peace was brought before it, the British member of the Council of Four always spoke on its behalf, and one of the Dominion Prime Ministers was often the second British representative on the Council of Ten. Sir Robert

Borden repeatedly presided over the British Empire delegation itself in the absence of the principal British delegate.' [1]

With the restoration of peace, however, this ideal method of conducting British Empire foreign policy, which had actually been practised for two years, became a counsel of perfection. In the states members of the British Commonwealth, as indeed in all countries in which the party system of responsible parliamentary government prevailed, home affairs normally preoccupied the minds of the electorate and therefore claimed the principal share of the attention of politicians ; and experience showed that, in countries so governed, hardly anything short of an actual state of war was potent enough to keep foreign affairs in the foreground of the political field of vision. Accordingly, the restoration of peace, as symbolized in the coming into force of the Versailles Treaty at the beginning of the year 1920, was the signal for a revulsion of interest from foreign to home affairs—a revulsion all the more violent on account of the comparative neglect of home affairs during the past half-dozen years. Among the people of every state member of the Commonwealth, not excluding Great Britain, there was manifest during the following years a desire to be left in peace in order to set the national house in order, and an impatience of any fresh alarums and excursions in the international field. This impatience was scarcely reasonable, since the formal conclusion of peace had by no means cleared up the aftermath of the War in the region which had been the scene of devastation, and had done little (notwithstanding the foundation of the League of Nations) to exorcise the danger of future wars in other parts of the world. The impatience existed, nevertheless, and made itself felt as a psychological factor of considerable importance in the conduct of British Empire foreign policy—the more so because it did not exert itself in the several states members of the Commonwealth with equal intensity. In Great Britain—chained by new bonds to the European Continent—it was not possible for the electorate to shut their eyes completely to the fact that the immense upheaval produced in Europe by the late War had not yet subsided. In the Overseas Dominions a statesman of the genius of General Smuts might discern that the cyclone had not been dissipated but had simply travelled from Europe to another region (the warning on this subject to which he gave public utterance at the Imperial Conference of 1921 has been quoted in the Introduction to this Part [2]) ; yet it was comparatively easy for the overseas electorates

[1] 'The Dominions and Foreign Policy,' a series of articles published in *The Times* (3rd February, 1925).   [2] See p. 30 above.

to cherish the agreeable delusion that they had now returned to that happy state of international isolation in which they had been living before 1914. Accordingly, from 1920 onwards, that method of communication and consultation by means of personal contact between Prime Ministers which had prevailed for two years was no longer possible.

During the seven years ending on the 31st December, 1926, there were only three plenary meetings of Prime Ministers—namely, the Imperial Conferences of 1921, 1923, and 1926—and these only lasted for 46, 39, and 36 days each respectively. Yet, even so, the absences from home which these meetings entailed for the overseas Prime Ministers were politically so inconvenient to them that it was evidently impossible to arrange that the Imperial Conference should meet less infrequently.[1] It is true that, on these three occasions, the Prime Ministers were able to settle certain very important matters of Imperial policy [2]—particularly during the Conference of 1921, at which it was found possible to reconcile the views of the South Sea Dominions and Canada with regard to the Anglo-Japanese Alliance and so to agree upon a common policy respecting the invitation from the President of the United States to attend the forthcoming international conference at Washington. Care was also taken that the meetings of the Imperial Conference, infrequent though they were, should render the most effective possible service to the cause of inter-Imperial co-operation by receiving a judicious publicity—a policy which was recommended by Mr. Meighen in 1921 [3] and again by Mr. King in 1923 [4] and which was duly carried out in 1923 and 1926.[5] Yet it was evident that inter-Imperial communication and consultation on foreign policy could not be confined to opportunities —however skilfully these might be used—which in the nature of the case in normal circumstances could only occur once in every two or every three years. The practical problem, therefore, was to supplement the sessions of the Imperial Conference by other methods of communication and consultation which, though inferior in other respects, would fulfil the indispensable requirement of continuity.

Already, during the War, the system of direct personal contact

[1] On this point, see the Introduction to this volume, pp. 34–5.

[2] In *The Dominions Office and Colonial Office List*, 1927, pp. lxvi-lxxvi, there is an admirable summary of the proceedings of the three Imperial Conferences of 1921, 1923, and 1926 (as well as the Imperial Economic Conference of 1923), and of the action taken on the resolutions of these conferences and on those of previous Imperial Conferences. The major part of the work done related, of course, to inter-Imperial relations, not to Empire foreign relations.

[3] See *Cmd.* 1474 of 1921, p. 17.   [4] See *Cmd.* 1988 of 1923, p. 13.

[5] See *Cmd.* 1987 of 1923, pp. 9–10 ; *Cmd.* 2768 of 1926, p. 12.

between Prime Ministers had been supplemented by direct written and telegraphic communications, for which special arrangements were in force from 1918 onwards.   Nevertheless, the ordinary channels of communication in peace time between the Governments of states members of the British Commonwealth remained notably less effective than the ' two-way ' personal channel which was provided, in the relations between sovereign and independent states, by the long established system of reciprocally accredited diplomatic representatives—an anomaly which aroused a certain uneasiness in the minds of many British statesmen and publicists.   A solution, however, was not easy to find, as was revealed by a correspondence [1] with the Governments of the self-governing Dominions (including Newfoundland), regarding consultation on matters of foreign policy and general Imperial interest, which was initiated by a circular telegram of the 23rd June, 1924, from His Majesty's Government in Great Britain, to the following effect :

23rd June.   Following from Prime Minister for your Prime Minister :
Begins :   You will probably have seen from Press reports of recent speeches of Secretary of State for the Colonies and myself in Parliament that we are concerned as to adequacy of present system of consultation with other self-governing parts of Empire on matters of foreign policy and general Imperial interest.   We fully accept principle of necessity for effective arrangements for continuous consultation in all important matters of common Imperial concern, and for such necessary concerted action, founded on consultation, as the several Governments may de-termine (see Resolution IX of Imperial War Conference, 1917).   We also realize that action to be taken as result of consultation whether at or between Imperial Conferences must be subject to constitutional require-ments of each country.   But we feel, as result of our experience since taking office, that system in practice has two main deficiencies.
First, it renders immediate action extremely difficult, more especially between Conferences, on occasions when such action is imperatively needed, particularly in sphere of foreign policy.
Secondly, when matters under discussion are subjects of political con-troversy, economic or otherwise, conclusions reached at and between Imperial Conferences are liable to be reversed through changes of Government.
Such a state of affairs inevitably leads to ineffectiveness ; it also causes disappointment, and doubts are thrown on utility of whole Imperial Conference system.
What the remedy is, it is difficult to say.   On the first point, i. e. the importance of securing, on occasion, rapid decisions, particularly on matters of foreign policy, it occurs to us that further examination of the Resolution on Negotiation, &c., of Treaties passed at last year's Imperial Conference [2] might be worth while in order to consider how

[1] Texts in *Cmd.* 2301 of 1925.   [2] See Section (v) (c) below.

far that Resolution needs to be supplemented and interpreted, and whether principles embodied in it can usefully be extended to other matters affecting foreign relations.

On the second point, i.e. means of making Imperial Conference Resolutions, whether they relate to economic or other matters, more effective, what is wanted is, I think, as I indicated in a speech in Parliament on 18th June, 'creation of some sort of workable machinery so that the public opinion of the whole of our Commonwealth of States should influence the policy for which the Commonwealth must be responsible.'

We had in view desirability of avoiding party issues when proposing appointment of Economic Committee with a reference framed so as to exclude questions of tariff policy.

One method of bringing about result desired which was mentioned by Secretary of State in recent speech in Parliament is that Imperial Conferences in future should not be confined to representatives of parties in office for time being. When it was contemplated some years ago that a special Constitutional Conference should be held, it was proposed from more than one quarter that such a Conference should be representative of Oppositions as well as Governments. On the other hand we realize that this suggestion is open to the criticism that it would tend to hamper the frank exchange of views and unrestricted inter-communication of confidential information on such matters as foreign policy and defence which have become so outstanding features of recent Conferences.

Another method might be to continue representation of Governments only but to arrange for each Government to obtain from its own Parliament beforehand a general approval, within sufficiently wide limits, of the attitude to be taken up by its representatives. Whilst avoiding the criticism of the first method, this might tend to diminish flexibility of Conference procedure.

We should like your views on these suggestions, and if you should be able to make any others they would be welcome. We ourselves have quite an open mind, and are merely exploring situation.

Our own feeling is that time has hardly come either to revive idea of Constitutional Conference or to call special meeting of Imperial Conference to consider problems outlined above. But we should like these problems given preliminary examination in near future and it has occurred to us that possible method might be to have a meeting of, say, two representatives of each country concerned who have had experience of constitutional working, to consider these problems and present a report as basis for further discussion. How would you view this idea, and, if it commends itself, what time would be most convenient for a meeting? Possibly October might be suitable as this would permit of some of Dominion delegates to next Assembly of League of Nations being amongst representatives if this were desired.

Similar telegram sent to other Prime Ministers.
RAMSAY MacDONALD. *Ends.*
—THOMAS.

The most constructive of the suggestions which were elicited by this telegram were contained in a message from the Prime Minister of Australia to the Prime Minister of Great Britain which was transmitted telegraphically on the 16th July, 1924, by the Governor-General of the Commonwealth to the Secretary of State for the Colonies in Whitehall.

It is, of course, obvious that in practice there are two main difficulties in establishment of an effective system of joint consultation and action, namely (a) the impossibility of full exchange of views when the Imperial Conference is not sitting, particularly in the sphere of foreign policy where immediate action is imperative, and (b) the possibility of conclusions of Imperial or Economic Conferences being reversed through change of government.

The problems which have to be considered appear to divide themselves into : (1) the manner in which an Imperial policy should be laid down in regard to matters of common Empire interest, such as foreign policy, defence, and inter-Empire trade. (2) How should consultations take place with regard to giving effect to such policy when determined upon and for its alteration where necessity arises ? (3) What steps can be taken to ensure that any common policy arrived at will be given effect to irrespective of change of government in different parts of the Empire ?

With regard to (1) it is now an established principle of Empire Government that Prime Minister Conferences shall take place at frequent intervals. At these Conferences a common Empire policy on questions of Imperial interest can be arrived at and submitted by the respective Prime Ministers to their individual Parliaments for their ratification and assent. The machinery for ensuring a common policy therefore already exists by holding of the Imperial Conferences, and no alteration of existing practice appears either necessary or desirable.

(2) It is unavoidable that questions of urgent foreign policy must be dealt with according to the circumstances in which they arise, and they are therefore in an entirely different category from other matters upon which a common policy may have been determined at an Imperial Conference. It appears to my Government therefore that no alteration in the underlying principle of consultation which at present exists is practicable, but considerable improvements could be effected in the operation of such machinery. These improvements should be on lines of (a) a closer liaison between the Foreign Office and Dominion Governments, which could be effected by the establishment by the Dominions of a Foreign Office Branch in their High Commissioners' Offices under the control of an officer of such standing and character as to enjoy the confidence of the Foreign Office ; such a representative would be in a position to keep his Prime Minister informed in regard to current events and atmosphere in connexion with foreign policy, in addition to information which is conveyed by cable to the Prime Minister and by information at present sent from time to time by the Foreign Office. (b) Fuller and more regular advice in regard to all questions of foreign affairs, both by cable and mail, than is at present forwarded to the Prime Ministers of the self-governing Dominions. (c) Greater efforts to anticipate questions which are likely to arise and require urgent

decision, with a view to ascertaining the views of the Dominions in advance in place of informing them of decisions after they have been arrived at and acted upon or when it is too late for any alternative action to be submitted.

With regard to questions other than foreign policy, my Government is of opinion that the establishment of a permanent Imperial Secretariat responsible to the Prime Ministers of all the self-governing parts of the Empire, whose task would be to prepare for the Imperial Conferences, carry out all Secretariat work during the sittings of such Conferences, follow up all Resolutions and decisions arrived at, and keep the Dominions constantly informed of developments between the Conferences, would go a long way towards solving the problem of effective and continuous consultation. This Secretariat would also embrace existing Imperial Committees such as the War Graves and Shipping, and the Economic Committee when established. It would not merely be a connecting link between the individual Dominion Governments and the British Government, but also between the Governments of the different Dominions. At the present time the Secretariat for Imperial Conferences is provided by the British Government, together with representatives of the Dominions concerned, but immediately the Conference is over the Secretariat is broken up, and no effective machinery exists for keeping the Dominions continuously informed as to developments or alterations necessitated by changed circumstances. In the opinion of my Government a great improvement would be effected by the establishment of a permanent Imperial Secretariat.

These Australian suggestions were acted upon by the Australian Government themselves as far as this lay in their power. In particular, they took two effective steps to establish a closer liaison with the Foreign Office. In 1924 they arranged with the Government at Westminster that a Foreign Office official of Australian birth, Mr. A. W. A. Leeper, should visit Australia, on a temporary mission, in order to advise upon ways and means of keeping the Prime Minister's Office there in touch with the Foreign Office by cable and mail ; and from the end of 1924 onwards they maintained in London, as a liaison officer for foreign affairs, a member of the staff of the Prime Minister's Office who corresponded directly and confidentially with that Office and with the Prime Minister himself.

As for the second suggestion made in Mr. MacDonald's message—regarding the possibility of promoting continuity in British Empire foreign policy by securing some representation, at Imperial Conferences, for oppositions, as well as for the parties momentarily in power in the respective states members of the Commonwealth—its practicability was questioned in the replies received from Australia and Newfoundland, while the Canadian Prime Minister, in a message of the 8th August, 1924, opposed it on the ground that it was open to a positive constitutional objection.

Proposal to have all parties represented in the Imperial Conferences with a view to preventing policy agreed upon thereat being rejected by existing or future Parliaments would seem to imply setting up a new body supreme over the several Parliaments. We regard the Imperial Conference as Conference of Governments of which each is responsible to its own Parliament and ultimately to its own electorate and in no sense as Imperial Council determining the policy of the Empire as a whole. We would deem it most inadvisable to depart in any particular from this conception, which is based on well-established principles of Ministerial responsibility and the supremacy of Parliament. We consider that with respect to all Imperial Conference resolutions or proposals each Government must accept responsibility for its attitude and the Opposition or Oppositions be free to criticize; with Parliaments and if occasion arises peoples deciding the issues.

Mr. MacDonald's proposal for a special meeting to discuss the questions raised in his message of the 23rd June, 1924, was also deprecated by the Australian Prime Minister in his message of the 16th July and by the South African Prime Minister in a message of the 21st August—the Australian Prime Minister's observations on the point being as follows :

We appreciate your attempt to explore the situation and agree as to the importance of finding a solution. We feel, however, that solution will be gradually evolved and consider that our object is more likely to be defeated than attained by undue precipitance.

The existing arrangements for the formation of a common Imperial policy and for subsequent consultation form the basis of a system which in the future may well become effective.

In these circumstances we do not see that any advantage is to be gained by the appointment of representatives to consider this problem and present a report as a basis for further discussion. All points at present under discussion were present to the minds of the Prime Ministers at the Imperial Conference held last year, but it was unanimously felt that the best course to pursue was to allow the situation to solve itself by gradual evolution rather than by immediate definite action.

My Government therefore does not propose to send representatives to a conference to discuss these questions, but is prepared during the interval until the next Imperial Conference is held to explore further any suggestions that may be put forward, and also to offer for similar consideration by other governments concerned any improvements in the existing machinery which may occur to us.

On the other hand, the Governments of New Zealand, Canada, Newfoundland, and the Irish Free State signified their willingness to send representatives to a meeting of the kind proposed; and ultimately the Australian and South African Governments waived their objections, though without enthusiasm. In these circumstances the proposal was withdrawn by Mr. Amery (the Secretary of State for the Colonies in the administration which succeeded Mr. Mac-Donald's), in a circular dispatch of the 2nd December, 1924, on grounds which practically coincided with those given in the Australian Prime Minister's message of the 16th July which has been quoted above. Mr. Amery added, however, that there was one pressing matter—namely the Geneva Protocol for the Pacific Settlement of International Disputes—on which personal consultation was, in the view of the Westminster Government, essential ; and with regard to the arrangements to be made for securing personal consultation on this matter he promised to communicate with the Dominion Prime Ministers at an early date. In the event, a special personal meeting proved too difficult to arrange for this purpose also, and the exchanges of views required for the establishment of a common policy regarding the Protocol as between states members of the Commonwealth had to be made by correspondence.[1]

The problem, thus left unsolved, of communication and consultation in the intervals between Imperial Conferences was taken up once more by the Inter-Imperial Relations Committee of the Conference of 1926, which reported as follows :

Sessions of the Imperial Conference at which the Prime Ministers of Great Britain and of the Dominions are all able to be present cannot, from the nature of things, take place very frequently. The system of communication and consultation between Conferences becomes therefore of special importance. We reviewed the position now reached in this respect with special reference to the desirability of arranging that closer personal touch should be established between Great Britain and the Dominions, and the Dominions inter se. Such contact alone can convey an impression of the atmosphere in which official correspondence is conducted. Development in this respect seems particularly necessary in relation to matters of major importance in foreign affairs where expedition is often essential, and urgent decision necessary. A special aspect of the question of consultation which we considered was that concerning the representation of Great Britain in the Dominions. By reason of his constitutional position, as explained in section iv (b) of this Report, the Governor-General is no longer the representative of His Majesty's Government in Great Britain. There is no one therefore in the Dominion capitals in a position to represent with authority the views of His Majesty's Government in Great Britain.

We summed up our conclusions in the following Resolution which is submitted for the consideration of the Conference :

The Governments represented at the Imperial Conference are impressed with the desirability of developing a system of personal contact, both in London and in the Dominion capitals, to supplement the present system of inter-communication and the reciprocal supply of information on affairs requiring joint consideration. The manner in

---

[1] See Survey for 1925, Vol. II, Part I A, Section (i).

which any new system is to be worked out is a matter for consideration and settlement between His Majesty's Governments in Great Britain and the Dominions, with due regard to the circumstances of each particular part of the Empire, it being understood that any new arrangements should be supplementary to, and not in replacement of, the system of direct communication from Government to Government and the special arrangements which have been in force since 1918 for communications between Prime Ministers.

It may be noted that this resolution applied not only to British Empire foreign policy but to Inter-Imperial affairs.

The Inter-Imperial Relations Committee further suggested that the general principle expressed in relation to treaty negotiations in their Report (in a passage which is quoted below under that head [1]), might usefully be adopted in future, as a guide, by the Governments concerned, in all negotiations affecting foreign relations falling within their respective spheres. The Committee observed that this principle was already to a large extent in force, and it appears to have been acted upon systematically after the Report had been adopted by the plenary Conference.

In the course of the next eighteen months certain steps were also taken, by the Governments of several states members of the Commonwealth, towards working out new practical arrangements for co-operation on the lines which the Inter-Imperial Relations Committee had contemplated.

The new system of direct communication between His Majesty's Government in Great Britain and the Dominions, without the intervention of the Governor-General of the Dominion concerned, was inaugurated, as between Great Britain and the Irish Free State, some time during the first half of the year 1927, and as between Great Britain and both Canada and South Africa on the 1st July, 1927. The Australian Government, which already had its liaison officer in London, was also in favour of the new system, but wished to inaugurate it at a later date. The New Zealand and Newfoundland Governments did not desire any change for the time being. Under the new system, communications from His Majesty's Government in Great Britain were sent to the Minister for External Affairs of the Dominion concerned instead of the Governor-General; but the Governor-General, while ceasing to be the political representative of His Majesty's Government in Great Britain, remained the personal representative of the King; and it was understood that, in this capacity, he was to be kept informed by the Government of the Dominion

[1] Section (v) (a) of the Report, quoted in Section (v) (c) of this part of the present volume.

regarding all questions, both internal and external, as fully as the King was kept informed by his Ministers in Great Britain.[1]

From the 1st July, 1927, when this new arrangement came into force as between the Governments of Great Britain and South Africa, the Government of Great Britain began to employ the Imperial Secretary to the British High Commissioner in South Africa,[2] Captain B. E. H. Clifford, to act as its spokesman in its direct dealings with the Government of the Union on occasions when it preferred the oral method of communication to that of the dispatch or the cable. Captain Clifford appears to have been definitely appointed to this duty at the beginning of the year 1928, but the fact was only announced (by General Hertzog in the South African House of Assembly) on the 25th April of that year.[3]

In January 1928 it was intimated by His Majesty's Secretary of State in Great Britain for Dominion Affairs, Mr. Amery, during a visit to Canada, that a representative of His Majesty's Government in Great Britain was to be appointed to perform a similar function at Ottawa, probably with the title of High Commissioner, on the analogy of the Dominion High Commissioners in London.[4]

On the 28th May, 1928, in the Canadian House of Commons, Mr. Bourassa moved an amendment (to a motion that the House go into Committee of Supply) regretting

that proper measures have not yet been taken to give clear effect in internal and external affairs to that equality of status recommended by the Imperial Conference of 1926 as a fundamental principle of the relations between the autonomous British communities.

The debate turned on the circumstances in which Canada had broken off relations with the U.S.S.R. at the time when Great Britain broke them off in 1927.[5] Mr. Bourassa's amendment was eventually withdrawn after the Prime Minister, Mr. Mackenzie King, had announced that if it were pressed to a division the Government would resist it as a motion of want of confidence.[6]

[1] For these facts see *The Times*, 2nd July, 1927.
[2] The office of British High Commissioner in South Africa had hitherto been combined in the same person as the office of Governor-General.
[3] *The Times*, 27th April, 1928; compare a reference in *The Times* of the 24th January, 1928, in the report of a statement made on the 23rd by Mr. Amery at Ottawa.
[4] *The Manchester Guardian*, 13th January, 1928; *The Times*, 23rd and 24th January, 1928. On this occasion, Mr. Amery appears to have deprecated the suggestion that this representative of one of His Majesty's Governments *auprès* another of His Majesty's Governments should have a diplomatic title or status.
[5] This will be dealt with in the *Survey for 1927*.
[6] See *The Times*, 30th and 31st May, 1928.

Meanwhile, the Government of New Zealand had arranged with the Government of Great Britain that a member of the staff of the Foreign Office with the seniority of a second secretary, Mr. P. B. B. Nichols, should 'be seconded for attachment to the Department of the Prime Minister of New Zealand in a consultative or informative capacity, especially in relation to foreign affairs'. Mr. Amery announced this appointment in the House of Commons at Westminster, in answer to a parliamentary question, on the 14th February, 1928. On the same occasion, he stated that Mr. Nichols would 'not exercise executive or administrative functions', and that he would not 'be in any sense a representative of His Majesty's Government in Great Britain.' His salary was to be borne on the Dominion Services Vote.[1] The closest precedent to Mr. Nichols's appointment was perhaps Mr. Leeper's mission to Australia in 1924.[2]

(b) The Representation of the British Empire at International Conferences (1919–26), and the Obligations of States Members of the Commonwealth in regard to Treaties resulting therefrom.

A new epoch in the constitutional history of the self-governing Dominions of the British Crown was opened by their representation at the Peace Conference of Paris in 1919.[3] How this came about may best be described in the words of Sir Robert Borden, a statesman who took a principal part in these transactions. In a speech delivered in the Canadian House of Commons on the 2nd September, 1919, he recorded that, after his arrival in London after the Armistice of the 11th November, 1918,

the status of the Dominions at the Peace Conference came immediately into question and was the subject of earnest discussion. Various methods, which it is not necessary to explain, were suggested. In the end I proposed that there should be a distinctive representation for each Dominion similar to that accorded to the smaller Allied Powers, and in addition that the British Empire representation of five delegates should be selected from day to day from a pool made up of the representatives of the United Kingdom and the Dominions. This proposal was adopted by the Imperial War Cabinet. . . . The preliminary Peace Conference began at Paris on January 12, and the question of procedure, including that of representation, was immediately taken up by the representatives of the Allied and Associated Powers. At first strong objection was made to the proposed representation of the British Dominions. Subsequently there was a full discussion in the British Empire Delegation, at which

[1] Statement by Mr. Amery in the House of Commons at Westminster on the 20th February, 1928.
[2] See p. 78 above.   [3] See *H. P. C.*, vol. vi, Ch. IV.

a firm protest was made against any recession from the proposal adopted in London. In the end that proposal was accepted.

The adoption of the panel system gave to the Dominions a peculiarly effective position. At plenary sessions there were sometimes three Canadian plenipotentiaries, two as representatives of Canada and one as representative of the Empire. Moreover, throughout the proceedings of the Conference the Dominion delegates, as members of the British Empire delegation, were thoroughly in touch with the proceedings of the Conference and had access to all papers. . . . Dominion Ministers were nominated to and acted for the British Empire on the principal Allied Commissions appointed by the Conference from time to time to consider and report upon special aspects of the conditions of peace. . . . During the last month of my stay in Paris I acted regularly as Chairman of the British Empire Delegation in the absence of the Prime Minister of the United Kingdom, whose duties as a member of the Council of Four constantly prevented his attendance.[1]

As a natural sequence it was determined upon the initiative of the Dominions that the consent of the Crown to the various treaties should in respect of the Dominions be expressed by the signature of their plenipotentiaries, and that the preamble and other formal parts of the treaties should be prepared accordingly. Thus the Dominions as signatories of the Peace Treaty became members of the League of Nations and acquired (at least *vis-à-vis* the other members of the League) a distinctive international status that they had not previously possessed. In accordance with constitutional usage the Peace Treaties were submitted to the Parliament of each Dominion for ratification, which did not take place until after the approval of each Parliament had been secured.[2]

The procedure thus established at the Paris Peace Conference in 1919 set a precedent for the procedure at the Washington Conference in 1921–2.

When the President of the United States in the autumn of 1921 issued the invitations to the Disarmament Conference at Washington, regret was expressed in one Dominion, at least, that an invitation had been extended to the Government of the United Kingdom alone, and that the status of the self-governing Dominions had not received due consideration. There were precedents for extending separate invitations to the Dominions. For example, in July 1911 an International Conference was summoned by the United States for revision of the International Convention respecting protection of industrial property. A special invitation to be present at that Conference was conveyed to the Government of Canada through the Ambassador at Washington and the Governor-General. However, in 1921 no such invitation was sent, and there was serious consideration as to whether certain Dominions would not stand aloof from the Conference, and decline to be bound by any treaty or convention there concluded. Having regard to the importance

[1] Sir Robert Borden in the Canadian House of Commons, 2nd September, 1919.

[2] Sir Robert Borden in *The Yale Review*, July 1923.

and significance of the Conference, it was wisely decided that the absence of a special invitation should be overlooked and that the Dominions should be represented at Washington by plenipotentiaries nominated on their behalf, to whom full powers should be issued under the same practice that had prevailed at Paris in 1919. In the result the wisdom of this course was entirely apparent. The status and distinctive consideration that the Dominions had received at Paris were accorded to them at Washington. There were regular meetings of the Commonwealth's delegates at which all important questions were discussed and determined in advance. In the formal parts of the treaties special representation of each Dominion was recognized, and each plenipotentiary of the Commonwealth signed on behalf of the Government that he represented.[1]

On the other hand, the precedent thus created at Paris and at least partially maintained at Washington was not followed at all in the composition of the British Empire Delegation at the Peace Conference between the Allied Powers and Turkey which was held at Lausanne in 1922–3 ; and this departure from precedent in the matter of representation at the Lausanne Conference led to difficulties over the ratification of the resulting Lausanne Peace Treaty in the case of one state member of the British Commonwealth, the Dominion of Canada.

Such a departure from a precedent by that time well established was particularly unfortunate in October 1922 [2]—a time at which, ' especially, care was required since the alarms raised by the Chanāq Incident [3] of a few weeks before had not died down '.[4] There is no

[1] Sir Robert Borden in *The Yale Review*, July 1923. It ought perhaps to be mentioned that the above interpretation of the constitutional and international significance of the British Empire representation at the Washington Conference was not undisputed. It was true that the ' full powers ' were issued in the same form for Washington as they had been for Paris, and that the signatures of the resulting agreements corresponded (as is shown by the fact that Lord Balfour signed them twice, once on behalf of His Majesty's Government in Great Britain and a second time on behalf of the Government of the Union of South Africa). At the same time, the proceedings at Washington appear to have differed from those at Paris in this, that at Washington the Dominions did not again obtain that dual representation which, at Paris, had given them a 'peculiarly effective position'. Although at Washington the Dominions were as effectively represented on the British Empire Delegation as they had been at Paris, they were not this time simultaneously represented by separate delegations of their own. On this point see Sir John Salmond's report to the New Zealand Government (N.Z. 1922, A. 5). See further a speech by General Smuts in the House of Assembly at Pretoria on the 18th July, 1922, reported in the *Journal of the Parliaments of the Empire*, 1922, p. 907.

[2] On this point, see the observations of Sir Edward Grigg in a speech in which he opened a debate on the subject in the House of Commons at Westminster on the 6th June, 1924.

[3] See Section (ii) above.   [4] *The Round Table*, September 1924, p. 810.

reason to suppose, however, that His Majesty's Government in Great Britain were not alive to this consideration, since the departure from precedent appears to have been made, not at their desire, but under pressure from France. The French Government are reported [1] to have offered opposition to the individual representation of the British self-governing Dominions at Lausanne except on condition that the non-self-governing French colonies and protectorates of Algeria,[2] West Africa, and Tunisia should also be represented on the same footing ; and the Westminster Government appears to have explained this confidentially to the Canadian Government at the time, as a reason why the individual representation of the Dominions at Lausanne had not been insisted upon. The first public statement, however, to this effect seems to have been made during a debate in the Canadian House of Commons on the 9th June, 1924.[3] The official message on the subject which was conveyed from His Majesty's Government in Great Britain to the Dominion Prime Ministers on the 27th October, 1922, merely announced certain arrangements which had been agreed upon already between the Governments of the three Principal Allied Powers, in the following terms :

Yesterday invitations were sent by Governments of Great Britain, France and Italy to the Japanese, Roumanian, Yugoslav, Greek and Turkish Governments (both of Constantinople and of Angora) to send representatives to Lausanne, 13th November, to conclude Treaty to end war in East, which would replace Treaty of Sèvres. Russian Soviet Government and Bulgarian Government also being invited to send to Lausanne, at a date to be fixed, representatives to take part in discussions on questions of the Straits, which the Conference will undertake at a later stage. Inquiry is also being addressed by the three Governments to the Government of the United States expressing hope that they will permit United States representative to be present during Lausanne negotiations in a capacity similar to that in which United States representative was present during negotiations at San Remo in 1920, or to take more active part in the negotiations specially on question of the Straits.

According to arrangements agreed upon with French and Italian Governments, each Government will be represented at Lausanne by two plenipotentiaries. Secretary of State for Foreign Affairs will personally act as Chief British Plenipotentiary, and it is proposed that he should be accompanied by British High Commissioner at Constantinople. Dominion Governments will be kept informed from time to time of the general lines of policy on which British plenipotentiaries propose to proceed, and of the course of negotiations, and, as in the case of the other Treaties arising out of the Peace Settlement, they will of course

[1] *The Round Table, num. cit., pag. cit.*
[2] A portion of Algeria enjoyed self-government, but as an integral portion of France and not as a separate self-governing community.
[3] *The Round Table, num. cit.,* p. 808.

be invited to sign new Treaty and any separate instruments regulating status of the Straits.

His Majesty's Government trusts that this procedure will be in accordance with the wishes of your Government.

British plenipotentiaries are fully acquainted with the Imperial aspect of the problem and with the keen interest taken by the Dominion Governments in its solution. Similar telegrams sent to other Prime Ministers.[1]

In reply to this telegram the Prime Minister of Canada, Mr. Mackenzie King, sent the following message to His Majesty's Government in Great Britain on the 31st October :

Our Government has no exception to take to the course pursued by His Majesty's Government with respect to the conclusion of a treaty to end the war in the Near East. As however it is proposed to keep our Government informed from time to time of the general lines of policy on which British plenipotentiaries propose to proceed and of the course of the negotiations and to invite us to sign a new treaty and any separate instrument regulating the status of the Straits, we deem it advisable to avail ourselves of the earliest opportunity to inform His Majesty's Government that in our opinion extent to which Canada may be held to be bound by the proceedings of the Conference or by the provisions of any treaty or other instrument arising out of the same is necessarily a matter for the Parliament of Canada to decide and that the rights and powers of our Parliament in these particulars must not be held to be affected by implication or otherwise in virtue of information with which our Government may be supplied.

This message would seem to imply that, as far as the peace settlement with Turkey was concerned, the Canadian Government had less desire to participate in the shaping of policy than to restrict the obligations of the Dominion, and to reserve the rights of the Dominion Parliament, in regard to whatever policy might emerge out of the Conference that was about to take place. His Majesty's Government in Great Britain replied on the 16th November that they fully understood that it was the desire of the Canadian Government that any treaty with Turkey which might result from the Lausanne Conference should be submitted to the Canadian Parliament for approval before the King was advised to ratify it, and that it was their most earnest desire that the Canadian Government should be kept informed of the developments of the Conference, of which they would endeavour to send full details. This message drew from the Canadian Prime Minister, on the 25th November, a further statement of the Canadian Government's point of view :

We feel that purport of my message of 31st October has not been correctly interpreted or understood. Our Government has not expressed

---

[1] *Correspondence with the Canadian Government on the subject of the Peace Settlement with Turkey (Cmd. 2146 of 1924).*

a desire to have any treaty with Turkey which may result from Conference submitted to Canadian Parliament for approval before His Majesty is advised to ratify it, nor do we wish to be understood as preferring any such request. My message was intended to make clear that we had no exception to take to Canada not being invited to be represented at the Conference, but, inasmuch as we had been informed that we would be invited to sign a new treaty and any separate instrument regulating status of Straits, we wished to make it perfectly clear that in our opinion extent to which Canada may be held to be bound by the proceedings of Conference or by provisions of any treaty or other instrument arising out of the same was necessarily a matter for the Parliament of Canada to decide. We deem it of utmost importance that there should be no misunderstanding as to our position with respect to Canada's obligations in this and kindred matters. In our opinion Parliament will desire as respects treaty with Turkey and any other instruments arising out of Lausanne Conference to reserve to itself the right to decide upon the merits of the case what action on the part of people of Canada is right and proper. In this connexion we shall be pleased to have authority to place before Parliament all the information with which we may from time to time be supplied.

In reply to this, His Majesty's Government in Great Britain explained that :

Our message of the 16th November was framed on assumption that Canadian Government would wish to follow procedure adopted in case of peace treaties with Germany, Austria and Bulgaria,

and set out as follows the position as it appeared to them :

Any treaty resulting from Lausanne Conference will, of course, replace Treaty of Sèvres, and until it comes into force a state of war between the British Empire and Turkey will technically continue. The Treaty must therefore be binding on the whole Empire when ratified. It remains to be seen whether there will be successful issue to Lausanne Conference, but if there is we should much prefer that any new Treaty should follow Paris precedent and include signatures on behalf of all the Dominions.

They added that they did not think that it would be possible to publish any of the telegrams which were then being sent to the Canadian Prime Minister regarding the proceedings at Lausanne, seeing that they often contained records of confidential interviews and impressions and other material intended for private information.

The reference, at the beginning of this message, to the ' procedure adopted in case of peace treaties with Germany, Austria, and Bulgaria ' drew from the Canadian Prime Minister, on the 31st December, 1922, a precise and lucid statement of what the precedents actually were :

Procedure referred to is, we understand, that adopted with respect to Paris Peace Conference, and followed later with respect to Washington Conference on the limitation of armament. As regards Canada's participation there were in that procedure four separate, distinct and essential stages.

1. Direct representation of Canada at the Conference at which treaties were drafted and participation in the proceedings of the Conferences by Canada's representatives, each representative holding a full power signed by His Majesty the King, in the form of Letters Patent, authorizing him to sign 'for and in the name of His Majesty the King, in respect of the Dominion of Canada ', any treaties, conventions or agreements that might tend to the attainment of the object of the Conference, the Canadian Government having, by Order in Council, sanctioned issuance of these full powers by His Majesty.

2. Formal signing of the treaties on behalf of Canada by the plenipotentiaries named.

3. Approval by the Parliament of Canada of the treaties thus signed on behalf of Canada.

4. Assent of the Government of Canada to the final act of ratification by His Majesty the King of the treaty signed on behalf of Canada approved by Parliament of Canada.

Your Grace is quite right in assuming that, as regards the treaties in which Canada is supposed to have a direct or immediate interest, the procedure here outlined is the one which our Government would wish to follow. In the case of main political treaties concluded since the War, in general rule seems to have been followed that, wherever the Dominions could be said to have a direct or immediate interest, the procedure was shaped to include their participation and signature of the proceedings. That in the case of the Conference at Lausanne a like procedure has not been followed with respect to representation and participation by Canada, has been regarded by us as evidence that, in the opinion of the countries by whom invitations to the Conference at Lausanne were extended, Canada could not have been believed to have the direct and immediate interest which she was supposed to have in the Conferences at Versailles and Washington.

To the course pursued with respect to Lausanne Conference we have, as mentioned in my telegram of 31st October, no exception to take. As regards the procedure, however, it must be apparent that quite apart from any action or representation on the part of the Government of Canada a different procedure has been followed in the case of the present Conference at Lausanne to that followed at Versailles and Washington. In so far as one stage in procedure is necessarily dependent upon the stage preceding, it is difficult to see how a like procedure can be followed. Canada has not been invited to send representatives to the Lausanne Conference, and has not participated in the proceedings of the Conference either directly or indirectly. Under the circumstances we do not see how as respects signing on behalf of Canada we can be expected, in the case of a new treaty or of any separate instrument regarding Straits, to follow the procedure adopted in the case of the treaties with Germany, Austria and Bulgaria.

In the light of this statement His Majesty's Government in Great Britain, on the 27th January, 1923, sent a message to the Prime

Minister of Canada that, in the circumstances, they were ' willing to fall in with his suggestion' that any treaties with Turkey resulting from the Conference should be signed ' only by the British pleni-potentiaries who ' had ' negotiated them ', if this were generally acceptable. The Governments of the other Dominions appear to have concurred ; and, as between the Governments of Great Britain and Canada, the understanding was confirmed by an exchange of telegrams of the 7th and 15th June, 1923.

The implications of this understanding, from the Canadian Govern-ment's point of view, were explained by Mr. Mackenzie King to his colleagues at the Imperial Conference which sat in London from the 1st October to the 8th November, 1923.

> In the presence of the Prime Ministers of the other Dominions and the members of the British Government I made it clear that because we were not represented and because we had no part in the Conference, this Government did not feel that it could bring into the House a Treaty negotiated as this Treaty had been negotiated, and expect to have the approval of Parliament of the obligations it carried with it. I made that clear, but I also made clear that we did not intend to embarrass the British Government in the matter when it came to the final ratification of the Treaty, and that whatever position the British Government might wish to take with regard to it, we would raise no objection. In other words, if the British Government recommended the ratification of the Treaty, so far as Canada was concerned, we were quite prepared that ratification should bind us. We never raised the question as to Canada not being bound by ratification.[1]

This point of view was reaffirmed by the Canadian Government several months later, when the question of ratifying the Lausanne Peace Treaty actually arose. Whereas the Governments of India, New Zealand, Australia, and South Africa had signified their con-currence in ratification by the 1st April, 1924, without apparently raising constitutional issues,[2] the Canadian Government took occa-sion to raise an issue of this character. In reply to telegrams of the 23rd February and the 21st March, 1924, from His Majesty's Govern-ment in Great Britain, requesting concurrence in the ratification of the Lausanne Treaty and Conventions, the Canadian Government caused the Governor-General to telegraph, on the 24th March, as follows :

> Canadian Government not having been invited to send representative to the Lausanne Conference and not having participated in the pro-

[1] Statement by Mr. Mackenzie King in the Canadian House of Commons on the 9th June, 1924.

[2] Statement by Mr. Ramsay MacDonald in the House of Commons at Westminster on the 1st April, 1924. The Irish Free State did not signify its concurrence in ratification until early in July 1924.

ceedings of the Conference either directly or indirectly and not being for this reason a signatory to the Treaty on behalf of Canada . . . my Ministers do not feel that they are in a position to recommend to Parliament approval of the Peace Treaty with Turkey and the Convention thereto. Without the approval of Parliament they feel that they are not warranted in signifying concurrence in the ratification of the Treaty and Convention. With respect to ratification, however, they will not take exception to such course as His Majesty's Government may deem it advisable to recommend.

In the same telegram, the Canadian Government expressed the opinion that their position appeared to be in harmony with the resolution of the recent Imperial Conference [1] (*Cmd.* 1987 of 1923, pp. 14 and 15), the provisions of which with reference to signature 2 (a) on p. 14 and to ratification (a) on p. 15 appeared to cover this case,[2] which did not come within the provisions of signature 2 (b) on p. 14 and ratification (b) on p. 15.

The policy of the Canadian Government in declining to lay the Lausanne Treaty before the Canadian Parliament, without at the same time declining to consent to the ratification of the treaty on the part of the British Empire, was clearly explained by Mr. Mackenzie King in the Canadian House of Commons on the 9th June, 1924.

There is a distinction to be drawn between the purely legal and technical position in which this Dominion may be placed and the moral obligations which arise under treaties, depending upon the manner in which such treaties are entered into, upon the parties who are present, and the representative capacities in which they acted while negotiations were proceeding. Legally and technically Canada will be bound by the ratification of this Treaty ; in other words, speaking internationally, the whole British Empire in relation to the rest of the world will stand as one when this Treaty is ratified. But as respects the obligations arising out of the Treaty itself, speaking now of inter-Imperial obligations, this Parliament, if regard is to be had to the representations which from the outset we have made to the British Government, will in no way be bound by any obligation beyond that which Parliament of its own volition recognizes as arising out of the situation.

We have not in the past, we do not now hold the view that Canada

[1] See Section (v) (c) below.
[2] The provisions here cited as applicable referred to ' bilateral treaties imposing obligations on one part of the Empire only ' while the provisions cited as not being applicable referred to ' treaties imposing obligations on more than one part of the Empire'. Later, the Canadian Government explained that, in this passage, it had intended to allude to the particular obligations of the Straits Convention. For a criticism of the formulae quoted in this footnote from the resolution of the Imperial Conference of 1923, see an article by Professor Sir W. Harrison Moore in the *Journal of Comparative Legislation* (Third Series, vol. viii, Part I). It may be noted that the term ' active obligations' was substituted for ' obligations' in the Report of the Inter-Imperial Relations Committee of the Imperial Conference of 1926.

as a part of the British Empire will not be legally bound by this Treaty when it is ratified, but we do say that the moral obligation resting upon this Parliament and country under this Treaty, when it is ratified, will be vastly different to the moral obligation which is imposed upon the country under the Treaty of Versailles, having regard to the different manner in which the whole negotiations were carried on.

This was, of course, simply an application—in the field of treaties negotiated at international conferences—of the distinction between automatically incurred (and therefore ' passive ') commitments and deliberately assumed (and therefore ' active ') responsibilities of states members of the British Commonwealth in the foreign relations of the British Empire—a distinction which had been formulated already in the matter of belligerency.[1]

The specific question of Dominion representation at international conferences arose again, a few weeks later, during the preparations for the London Reparations Conference of the 16th July—16th August, 1924, when a preliminary meeting of delegates of Great Britain and the Dominions was held in order to arrange for representation at the Conference itself. The proceedings at this meeting were described by Mr. Mackenzie King in the Canadian House of Commons on the 17th July, 1924, as follows :

In order that there might be no mistake in our position in the matter of representation we intimated immediately that, in our opinion, representation, according to the terms of the resolution passed at the last Imperial Conference, should follow the precedents set at Versailles and Washington, whereby each Dominion would be separately represented by its delegate, bearing full powers from His Majesty to act, as respects the Dominion, in the name of His Majesty. In reply to that communication an intimation was given by the British Prime Minister that he was unable to say whether he could place the same interpretation upon the application of the resolution of the Imperial Conference as we placed upon it. It was, however, suggested that the representatives should meet and confer and the question of representation be decided as the result of the conference.

At the preliminary conference . . . it was intimated that it would not be possible for more than three representatives of the British Empire to be present at the inter-Allied Conference, and the dispatch rather suggested that the three in question would necessarily be members of His Majesty's Government. We intimated that this would not be satisfactory to the Dominion ; that, in our opinion, this Parliament would expect that the precedents set at Versailles and Washington should be followed and that our Government would expect that a Canadian representative with full powers from His Majesty in respect of Canada should represent this country as a member of the British Empire delegation. We drew attention to the fact that the internal

---

[1] See Section (ii) above.

organization of the British Empire delegation was a matter, in our opinion, for the British Empire itself to decide ; that any objection from other nations as to the manner in which representation was arranged within the Empire was something that was none of their affair. . . . My opinion is that there will probably be no difficulty in arranging for Canada's representation in the manner I have described.

' It was found impossible to arrive at definite arrangements before the Inter-Allied Conference opened ; '[1] and at the first plenary session of the Conference, which was held on the 16th July, 1924, the Dominions were not directly represented ;[2] but on the 18th July the Secretary of State for the Colonies, Mr. J. H. Thomas, made the following statement in the House of Commons at Westminster :

> I have now the great pleasure of announcing that it has been settled that representatives of any of the Dominions so desiring, and of India, shall become members of the British Empire Delegation at the Conference on the panel system, and it has also been arranged for the representatives so appointed to be present at the meetings of the Conference on days when it is not their turn to sit as members of the British Empire Delegation. This will ensure that they are fully acquainted with all that goes on in the Conference. The plan adopted is a special one for this particular Conference and is not to be regarded or quoted as a precedent.

From Mr. Thomas's replies to oral questions following upon this statement, it appeared that the delay had been due to difficulties in obtaining the consent of Canada to an arrangement in which the other Dominions had concurred with His Majesty's Government in Great Britain. From the 18th July onwards, however (i. e. during the whole course of the Conference save the first plenary session), the Dominions and India[3] were duly represented in accordance with the plan which Mr. Thomas had announced ; and, in addition, the whole panel of delegates from Great Britain, the Dominions, and India, from which the British Empire Delegation at the Conference was drawn, held a plenary private meeting every day while the Conference lasted, at which they discussed ' the whole situation, not as British delegates *versus* Dominions, but as one united delegation having a common interest '.[4]

[1] Statement by the Secretary of State for the Colonies, Mr. J. H. Thomas, in the House of Commons at Westminster on the 18th July, 1924, quoted below. [2] *The Times*, 17th July, 1924.

[3] The communities in the British Empire to which ' full powers ' were issued separately for the London Conference of 1924 appear to have been those which had received ' full powers ' for the Peace Conference of Paris (i. e. the four overseas Dominions and India, but not the Irish Free State) —the reason being that the London Conference was regarded as a sequel to the Paris Conference.

[4] See statements made by Mr. Thomas in the House of Commons at Westminster, in answer to parliamentary questions, on the 21st and 29th July, 1924.

With regard to the reservation that the plan adopted on this occasion was not to be regarded as a precedent, it is to be noted that the separate representation of the Dominions and India on British Empire Delegations at international conferences had, in fact, been described as ' the now established practice '[1] in a resolution on the negotiation, signature, and ratification of treaties which had been unanimously approved by the Imperial Conference of 1923.[2] In the light of the same resolution, the question of the representation of the different parts of the British Empire at international conferences was studied by the Inter-Imperial Relations Committee of the Imperial Conference of 1926, who summarized their conclusions as follows :

1. No difficulty arises as regards representation at conferences convened by, or under the auspices of, the League of Nations. In the case of such conferences all members of the League are invited, and if they attend are represented separately by separate delegations. Co-operation is ensured by the application of paragraph I. 1 (c) of the Treaty Resolution of 1923.

2. As regards international conferences summoned by foreign Governments, no rule of universal application can be laid down, since the nature of the representation must, in part, depend on the form of invitation issued by the convening Government.

   (a) In conferences of a technical character, it is usual and always desirable that the different parts of the Empire should (if they wish to participate) be represented separately by separate delegations, and where necessary efforts should be made to secure invitations which will render such representation possible.

   (b) Conferences of a political character called by a foreign Government must be considered in the special circumstances of each individual case.

It is for each part of the Empire to decide whether its particular interests are so involved, especially having regard to the active obligations likely to be imposed by any resulting treaty, that it desires to be represented at the Conference, or whether it is content to leave the negotiation in the hands of the part or parts of the Empire more directly concerned and to accept the result.

If a Government desires to participate in the conclusion of a treaty, the method by which representation will be secured is a matter to be arranged with the other Governments of the Empire in the light of the invitation which has been received.

Where more than one part of the Empire desires to be represented, three methods of representation are possible :

   (i) By means of a common plenipotentiary or plenipotentiaries, the issue of Full Powers to whom should be on the advice of all parts of the Empire participating.

[1] *Cmd.* 1987 of 1923, p. 14.   [2] See Section (v) (c) below.

(ii) By a single British Empire delegation composed of separate representatives of such parts of the Empire as are participating in the conference. This was the form of representation employed at the Washington Disarmament Conference of 1921.

(iii) By separate delegations representing each part of the Empire participating in the conference. If, as a result of consultation, this third method is desired, an effort must be made to ensure that the form of invitation from the convening Government will make this method of representation possible.

Certain non-technical treaties should, from their nature, be concluded in a form which will render them binding upon all parts of the Empire, and for this purpose should be ratified with the concurrence of all the Governments. It is for each Government to decide to what extent its concurrence in the ratification will be facilitated by its participation in the conclusion of the treaty, as, for instance, by the appointment of a common plenipotentiary. Any question as to whether the nature of the treaty is such that its ratification should be concurred in by all parts of the Empire is a matter for discussion and agreement between the Governments.[1]

At the International Conference on Naval Disarmament which sat at Geneva from the 20th June to the 4th August, 1927, the third of the three alternative methods of representation set out in the Report of the Inter-Imperial Relations Committee of 1926 was adopted—each part of the Empire participating in the conference being represented by a separate delegation. Thereby the equality of status of the states members of the British Commonwealth, which had been reciprocally recognized by those communities themselves at the Imperial Conference of 1926, obtained an implicit recognition of an international character, since at this international conference the Dominions were represented on a footing of equality not only with their fellow member of the Commonwealth, Great Britain, but with two foreign Powers, the United States and Japan.

Nevertheless, when the history of the representation of the British Empire at international conferences was considered in retrospect from the Paris Peace Conference of 1919 to the Geneva Naval Conference of 1927 inclusive, it could not be said that, by the latter date, this most important and most difficult problem had been satisfactorily solved. It might be granted that the procedure which had been devised and applied at Paris had been proved on its merits to be the best ; but when the pertinent question was asked why this procedure, which had justified itself at Paris and had been repeated in substance at Washington and then again at Geneva, had been

[1] *Cmd.* 2768 of 1926, pp. 24–5. It was evident, of course, that, under either method (ii) or method (iii), small informal meetings might take place which would not be attended by all the delegates.

departed from, in the interval between the Washington and the Geneva Naval Conferences, at the Peace Conference of Lausanne and at the Reparations Conference of London, it was not a sufficient answer to arraign His Majesty's Government in Great Britain, or their permanent officials in Whitehall, for relapsing into ' the methods of Downing Street '.

His Majesty's Government in Great Britain were able to show that, if they had relapsed, they had done so not out of perversity but under pressure. In the case of the Lausanne Conference, pressure was reported to have been applied by another European Government,[1] and the brunt of such pressure naturally had to be borne by His Majesty's Government in Great Britain which, for geographical and historical reasons, represented the British Commonwealth of Nations in Europe and served as the buffer between Continental European Governments and the Governments of the Dominions and India overseas. Yet even this answer was not the end of the matter ; for it still had to be explained why European Powers did not exercise with effect a similar pressure at the Paris Peace Conference or the United States at the Washington and Geneva Naval Conferences. It was no secret that the special representation of the self-governing communities of the British Empire at international conferences was not looked upon with favour by foreign Powers, which were apt to suspect the British Empire of exploiting the admitted peculiarity of its internal structure in order to obtain a more ample representation than was its due. Yet the ' strong objection ' which had been made to the special representation of the Dominions at Paris had been overcome ; [2] and when the President of the United States had pointedly issued an invitation for the Washington Conference to the United Kingdom alone, the special representation of the Dominions had nevertheless been secured at Washington, on a basis only less favourable than that which had been established at Paris, by the simple expedient of ignoring the form in which the invitation had been received.[3] In these two cases, therefore, the pressure from foreign Powers had not been pressed home ; and in the case of the London Reparations Conference—one of the two cases in which the precedents of Paris and Geneva had been departed from—there was evidence that the pressure upon His Majesty's Government in Great Britain, to which that departure was due, had been something more than pressure from other Powers.

We were faced [said Mr. Thomas, the Colonial Secretary of the day] with the conclusions of the Dawes Report. [And] . . . here you have

[1] See p. 86 above.   [2] See p. 83 above.   [3] See p. 85 above.

the real difficulty when you get such a situation as faced us in that Report. To bring the Dominions, to give them the same representation as we determined on at Versailles, meant that they themselves were to have six representatives. Any one with any knowledge of the European difficulty arising out of the Dawes Report would admit that we could not turn that Conference into a mass meeting. If you were going to be businesslike, you had to make it as small as possible, and the difficulty of that was not only our own difficulty but the difficulty of the other Powers represented. We immediately applied ourselves to the difficulty. We cabled to the Dominions, and said to them : ' Here is our difficulty. We want you to have the same representation as at Versailles, but there is a difficulty for this Conference. Will you help us ? ' During the whole of these negotiations we made it perfectly clear to them that on no consideration would they be committed in any way by any representatives of the British Government without full discussion and agreement. They all accepted it readily with the exception of Canada. We may as well be perfectly frank in this matter. The strength of the British Empire is that we can be frank with each other without unpleasantness. Mr. Mackenzie King, speaking for his Government, was frank. He said, ' No. I believe that accepting anything less than the principle agreed at Versailles is lowering our status '.[1]

This statement suggests the ultimate source of the pressure to which His Majesty's Government in Great Britain were subject. It was a pressure which arose, in the last analysis, not from the policy of other Powers but from the objective facts of the international situation as it happened to stand at the moment ; and the true answer to the question why the precedent of Paris was followed more or less closely at Washington and Geneva but was not followed at Lausanne and London is to be found in a fundamental difference in the circumstances in which these two sets of conferences were respectively convened.

On the eve of both the Lausanne and the London Conferences, the pressure of the international situation was acute. If the opening of the Lausanne Conference had been delayed, there might have been a recrudescence of the General War ; if the opening of the London Conference had been delayed, the economic situation in Germany might have taken another grave and perhaps irreparable turn for the worse. In either case, there were immediate possibilities of the utmost gravity ; and in such a situation it was morally almost impossible for His Majesty's Government in Great Britain to take upon themselves the responsibility for occasioning delay by insisting upon a particular form of representation for the British Empire— a form which to the world at large (unfamiliar, as it was, with the facts of ' Dominion Status ') would appear in the light either of

[1] *Hansard* (House of Commons), 29th July, 1924.

H

a pedantic point of procedure or else of an excessive pretension upon which it was unpardonable for any Government to insist at so great a risk to the general interests of mankind. Thus, in the preliminary discussions regarding British Empire representation on the eve of the Lausanne and the London Conferences, His Majesty's Government in Great Britain found themselves in a quandary between the pressure of the international situation on the one hand (a pressure of which a foreign Power appears to have taken diplomatic advantage on at least one of the two occasions), and the insistence of certain of the Dominions, on the other hand, upon the preservation of rights which they regarded themselves as having acquired at Paris in 1919 once for all. It was not to the discredit of His Majesty's Government in Great Britain that, in this dilemma, they twice took a course which safeguarded the international situation at the risk of imposing a strain upon British inter-Imperial relations.

There is an instructive contrast between the international situations which forced the hand of His Majesty's Government in Great Britain in regard to the Conferences of Lausanne and London and the situations which existed on the eve of the Conferences of Paris, Washington, and Geneva. At Paris, in contrast to Lausanne, the Allied and Associated Powers were meeting, not to negotiate a peace with an enemy who might resume hostilities at any moment if negotiations were delayed, but to dictate a peace to enemies who were militarily prostrate and impotent to resume hostilities for an indefinite time to come. At Paris, therefore, there was a sufficient margin of security for an important question of procedure to be threshed out between the parties before the substantive business of the Conference was set on foot. Again, at Washington and Geneva, though the substantive questions awaiting discussion were big with issues of peace or war, those issues were not yet imminent, and it was therefore possible for either of these conferences to be delayed or even to break down—as the Geneva Conference did in fact break down—without precipitating an immediate catastrophe. Accordingly, His Majesty's Government did not on these occasions find themselves under the same pressure to waive their claims in regard to British Empire representation as they did on the eves of the Conferences of Lausanne and London.

There was thus a clear correspondence between the respective international situations in which these two sets of Conferences were convened and the respective success or failure of His Majesty's Government in Great Britain in securing that representation for the British Empire which, in the unanimous opinion of all the self-governing communities in the Empire, including Great Britain herself, had been proved to be the best on its merits ; and this meant that the problem of British Empire representation at international conferences had not yet been solved completely. It would remain unsolved so long as the procedure which had been devised and applied at Paris in 1920 remained subject to being set aside under pressure from the international situation of the moment or even under pressure from foreign Governments on the watch to turn the international situation to diplomatic advantage. In the House of Commons at Westminster, on the 29th July, 1924, this delicate matter was touched upon by the Secretary of State for the Colonies, Mr. Thomas, in the following words :

> We want outsiders to understand that these domestic differences are not going to weaken us. They are inclined to take advantage of these difficulties. They are inclined to gloat over the kind of discussions that took place a few weeks ago over this Conference. We want them all plainly to understand that they are not going to take advantage of these difficulties, because we are going to remedy them in the future.

(c) THE NEGOTIATION, SIGNATURE AND RATIFICATION OF INTERNATIONAL TREATIES AND AGREEMENTS NOT ISSUING OUT OF INTERNATIONAL CONFERENCES[1]

In the preceding section, some account has been given of the constitutional problem which arose over the obligations of states members of the British Commonwealth in respect of treaties resulting from international conferences to which the British Empire was a party. In this age, however, most treaties issued, not out of international conferences, but out of bilateral negotiations conducted between Governments through the normal and permanent channels of international intercourse ; and bilateral negotiations with foreign countries, resulting in treaties or agreements, were frequently conducted by the British self-governing Dominions on their own account.

Indeed, in the case of commercial and technical treaties and agreements, at any rate (and the great majority of international treaties and agreements belonged to this category), the treaty-making power was inherent in Dominion Status, since the essence of Dominion self-government was that the Parliament of any given Dominion should enjoy the same powers in respect of that Dominion as were possessed by the Parliament at Westminster in respect of

[1] See an article on ' The Dominions and Treaties ' by Sir William Harrison Moore in the *Journal of Comparative Legislation and International Law*, Third Series, vol. viii, Part I, February 1926.

Great Britain and the non-self-governing parts of the British Empire —a definition of powers which evidently implied full parliamentary control over fiscal affairs and therefore the right of the Executive responsible to a Dominion Parliament to negotiate such treaties and agreements with foreign countries as might be necessary for the exercise of such fiscal control by Parliament in an effective manner.

The exercise of the treaty-making power by Dominion Governments in accordance with this unquestioned right gave rise to two problems, one of procedure and the other of obligation.

The (less important) problem of procedure arose from the fact that the normal and permanent channels of international intercourse that had long existed between the Governments of sovereign independent states had hardly yet begun to be established as between the Governments of states members of the British Commonwealth, other than Great Britain herself, and those of foreign countries. The first diplomatic representative accredited by His Britannic Majesty to a foreign Government on behalf of a self-governing Dominion of the British Crown presented his credentials on the 7th October, 1924 ; [1] the first accredited by a foreign state to His Britannic Majesty in the capital of a self-governing Dominion presented them on the 1st June, 1927 ; [2] and even then it seemed likely that a long time would elapse before a complete network of diplomatic relations would be woven between each self-governing Dominion and every foreign country with which it might desire to enter into direct negotiations. Hence the bilateral treaties and agreements negotiated by Dominion Governments with foreign Governments were not only made in the name of His Britannic Majesty (who was the juridical head of the state in each state member of the British Commonwealth as well as in the British Empire as a whole), but were conducted with the assistance of the diplomatic service which was maintained in foreign capitals by the Foreign Office in Whitehall.[3]

From this beginning, the treaty-making power of the Dominion Governments developed in two directions. There was a tendency for the Dominion authorities to play a greater and the representatives of the Foreign Office a smaller part in treaty negotiations initiated by Dominion Governments ; and there was also a tendency for Dominion Governments to enter into such negotiations with foreign

---

[1] See above, p. 66.   [2] See above, p. 66.

[3] The association of a Dominion representative with a representative of the Foreign Office occurred as far back as 1871, when the Treaty of Washington was negotiated and signed by a delegation which included Sir John Macdonald. There were, however, no differences in the full powers issued to the plenipotentiaries, and they acted strictly as a single delegation.

Governments over matters extending beyond the bounds of the commercial and technical field.

The second of these tendencies may be illustrated by the transfer of the treaty-making power from Great Britain to the Dominions in the case of international controversies over fisheries in which the chief British interests at stake were those of some self-governing Dominion and not those of Great Britain or the non-self-governing parts of the British Empire. In this sphere, in which political and territorial as well as commercial and technical questions were involved, a notable development took place within a period of twenty years. When the long-standing controversy between the British Empire and France over French fishing-rights in British territorial waters off Newfoundland—a controversy in which the interests of the self-governing colony of Newfoundland were the chief British interests at stake—had been settled by the negotiation and signature of the convention of the 8th April, 1904, the negotiations had been conducted by the Foreign Office in Whitehall and the resulting instrument had been signed, for the British Empire, by a representative of His Majesty's Government in Great Britain ; so that, although the Government of Newfoundland was consulted by the Government in Great Britain while the negotiations were in progress, the Newfoundland authorities did not take a direct part, either in form or in practice, in the proceedings. On the other hand, when certain questions outstanding with the United States with regard to the halibut fishery in the North Pacific Ocean were settled by the negotiation and signature of a treaty on the 2nd March, 1923, the negotiations were conducted on His Britannic Majesty's behalf by the Canadian Minister of Marine and Fisheries, Mr. Lapointe, and the instrument was signed, in His Majesty's name, by Mr. Lapointe alone.

This was an innovation in procedure, since ' in the past, when a Dominion ' had ' negotiated a separate commercial treaty with a foreign Power, the British Ambassador accredited to such Power ' had ' signed the treaty in association with the Dominion representative ' ; [1] and this procedure had been followed as lately as 1921 in the trade agreement of that year between Canada and France. The only agreements with foreign countries which down to that time had been signed as well as negotiated by Dominion representatives alone had been informal agreements such as that concluded between Canada and the United States in 1911 ; and these constituted no

[1] Mr. M. M. Lewis in *The British Year Book of International Law*, 1923–4, p. 168.

exception to the prevailing practice since they imposed no obligation on the Imperial Government and a breach of them was no ground for diplomatic representations.[1] On the other hand, ' in the course of the preliminary correspondence relating to the signing of the Halibut Treaty, the Governor-General of Canada telegraphed to the British Ambassador at Washington on the 21st February, 1923 :

> My Ministers are of opinion that as regards Canada the signature of Mr. Lapointe will be sufficient, and that it will not be necessary for you to sign as well.

To this the Ambassador replied on the 23rd February :

> I have been instructed by His Majesty's Government to sign the treaty in association with Mr. Lapointe.[2]

' But in consequence of further representations by the Canadian Government to the effect that the treaty affected solely the United States and Canada, the Imperial Government withdrew from its position, and the treaty was signed on the 2nd March by Mr. Hughes, the United States Secretary of State, and Mr. Lapointe. Thus for the first time a treaty was not only negotiated by a Dominion representative alone but also signed by him alone.'[3] On the 8th March, it was stated in the House of Commons at Westminster by the Prime Minister, in answer to a parliamentary question, that

> the plenipotentiary who signs a treaty does so as the representative of the King, by whom his full powers are issued, and the Canadian Minister acted in that capacity on the present occasion.

The Prime Minister did not go on to state whether the full power issued by the King on this occasion had been issued on the advice and authority of his ministers in Great Britain (as in the case of commercial treaties previously negotiated by Dominion Governments), or on that of his ministers in Canada (as in the case of the four European Peace Treaties of 1919–20).[4] In the printed text, however, which was eventually laid on the table of the House of Commons at Westminster,[5] the instrument was entitled a ' treaty

---

[1] Mr. M. M. Lewis, *op. cit.*, *loc. cit.*, quoting a letter from Professor A. Berriedale Keith which was published in *The Times* on the 19th March, 1923.

[2] A detailed account of the correspondence is given in ' Empire Foreign Policy ', by J. A. R. Marriott, in the *Fortnightly Review*, May 1923.

[3] Mr. M. M. Lewis, *loc. cit.*

[4] A parliamentary question on this specific point on the 19th March, 1923, failed to elicit any information from the Prime Minister beyond the statement that ' the arrangement made was the result of agreement between the two Governments '. A further question on the 23rd March was parried by reference to this reply.

[5] *Cmd.* 2377 of 1925.

between Canada [*sic*] and the United States of America for securing the preservation of the Halibut Fishery of the North Pacific Ocean '.

While the smaller question of procedure in respect of the treaty-making power had thus been raised as between Canada and Great Britain, the larger question of obligation was raised, over the same treaty, as between the British Empire and the United States. On this point, it is to be noted that the full power issued by the King to Mr. Lapointe on this occasion was ' the ordinary unqualified full power, containing no mark of any limitation of Mr. Lapointe's representative character, or indication that he signed in any other capacity than would have been filled if the British Ambassador had signed with him, or alone '.[1] It is also to be noted that the instrument was eventually ratified by the King under the Great Seal of the United Kingdom on the advice of one of his Secretaries of State in Great Britain (in whatever capacity that advice might be held to have been tendered).[2] Moreover on the 4th March, 1923, the United States Senate advised ratification of the treaty ' subject to the understanding that

> none of the nationals or inhabitants on boats or vessels of any other part of Great Britain [*sic*] shall engage in the halibut fishery contrary to the provisions of the Treaty.

And it is worthy of note that both the President of the United States and the Secretary of State referred to the treaty as being concluded not with Canada but with Great Britain.' [3]

In taking this action, the United States Senate showed that some circumstance—either the formal innovation consisting in the

---

[1] Sir William Harrison Moore in *The Journal of Comparative Legislation and International Law*, Third Series, vol. viii, Part I, p. 23. Cf. Professor Berriedale Keith in *op. cit.*, vol. v, Part IV, p. 166.

[2] Sir W. H. Moore, *loc. cit.*, pp. 22–4.

[3] Mr. M. M. Lewis, *loc. cit.* In the United States *Statutes at Large* (Vol. 43, Part 2), the document was headed : 'Convention between the United States and Great Britain for the preservation of the Halibut Fishery of the Northern Pacific Ocean'; and in the proclamation in which President Coolidge announced the exchange of ratifications on the 22nd October, 1924, the text of the treaty was preceded by the following preamble:
'Whereas a convention between the United States of America and Great Britain for the preservation of the halibut fishery of the Northern Pacific Ocean, including Bering Sea, was concluded and signed by their respective Plenipotentiaries at Washington on the second day of March, one thousand nine hundred and twenty-three. . . .'
It may be noted that in the interval the convention had come before the Senate of the United States a second time. The Senate had advised ratification on the 31st May, 1924, and the convention had been ratified by the President on the 4th June, 1924.

omission of the British Ambassador's signature or the substantial innovation consisting in the fact that the treaty negotiated between the United States and Canada in this case extended to political and territorial as well as to commercial and technical questions—had drawn attention at Washington to the mystery of the multiplicity in unity of the British Empire ; and this action on the part of a foreign legislative body served as a reminder to the statesmen of the British Commonwealth that, in so far as British inter-Imperial relations were concerned with the foreign relations of the British Empire, the self-determination of the states members of the Commonwealth was conditioned, not only by their attitudes *vis-à-vis* one another, but by the attitudes of foreign countries towards each and all of them.

This incident, together with the contemporary correspondence between Ottawa and Westminster regarding the conclusion of a peace treaty with Turkey,[1] led to an investigation into the whole subject of the negotiation, signature, and ratification of treaties when the Imperial Conference met in London on the 1st October of the same year 1923.

An authoritative account of the then existing practice, so far as Canada was concerned, may be found in the following statement by Sir Robert Borden, which had been published that July :

> Since the beginning of the present century, Canada has in many instances negotiated treaties that concerned her special interests. In such cases the diplomatic unity of the Commonwealth is preserved by the form of the treaty and by the method of execution and ratification.
>
> The King is named in the treaty as the High Contracting Party and the execution is under powers issued by him upon the recommendation of the Dominion Government. Ratification takes place also upon the recommendation of the Dominion Government ; but any relevant question as to the effect of the treaty upon the Commonwealth as a whole must naturally be the subject of consultation between the Governments concerned, prior to ratification. It is not improbable that in this respect usage, arising out of practice and experience as to the proper character, method and extent of such consultation, will develop into a recognized convention. There seems no reason to desire or to anticipate any modification in the form of such treaties. The ancient formula, by which the King is designated as the enacting authority, still subsists in the Statutes of each Dominion and in those of Great Britain ; in form the King, in reality the Legislative, enacts.[2]

At the Imperial Conference of 1923 the subject was examined officially by a committee consisting of representatives of the Five Dominions, Newfoundland, and India, under the chairmanship of

---

[1] See Section (v) (b) above.
[2] *The Yale Review*, July 1923.

the British Secretary of State for Foreign Affairs; and this committee drew up and agreed to the following resolution : [1]

The Conference recommends for the acceptance of the Governments of the Empire represented that the following procedure should be observed in the negotiation, signature and ratification of international agreements.

The word ' treaty ' is used in the sense of an agreement which, in accordance with the normal practice of diplomacy, would take the form of a treaty between Heads of States, signed by plenipotentiaries provided with Full Powers issued by the Heads of the States, and authorizing the holders to conclude a treaty.

I

1. *Negotiation.*

(*a*) It is desirable that no treaty should be negotiated by any of the Governments of the Empire without due consideration of its possible effect on other parts of the Empire, or, if circumstances so demand, on the Empire as a whole.

(*b*) Before negotiations are opened with the intention of concluding a treaty, steps should be taken to ensure that any of the other Governments of the Empire likely to be interested are informed, so that, if any such Government considers that its interests would be affected, it may have an opportunity of expressing its views, or, when its interests are intimately involved, of participating in the negotiations.

(*c*) In all cases where more than one of the Governments of the Empire participates in the negotiations, there should be the fullest possible exchange of views between those Governments before and during the negotiations. In the case of treaties negotiated at International Conferences, where there is a British Empire Delegation, on which, in accordance with the now established practice, the Dominions and India are separately represented, such representation should also be utilized to attain this object.

(*d*) Steps should be taken to ensure that those Governments of the Empire whose representatives are not participating in the negotiations should, during their progress, be kept informed in regard to any points arising in which they may be interested.

2. *Signature.*

(*a*) Bilateral treaties imposing obligations on one part of the Empire only should be signed by a representative of the Government of that part. The Full Power issued to such representative should indicate the part of the Empire in respect of which the obligations are to be undertaken, and the preamble and text of the treaty should be so worded as to make its scope clear.

(*b*) Where a bilateral treaty imposes obligations on more than one part of the Empire, the treaty should be signed by one or more plenipotentiaries on behalf of all the Governments concerned.

(*c*) As regards treaties negotiated at International Conferences, the

[1] Text in *Cmd.* 1987 of 1923, pp. 13–14, and in *Cmd.* 2768 of 1926, pp. 20–1.

existing practice of signature by plenipotentiaries on behalf of all the Governments of the Empire represented at the Conference should be continued, and the Full Powers should be in the form employed at Paris and Washington.

3. *Ratification.*

The existing practice in connexion with the ratification of treaties should be maintained.

II

Apart from treaties made between Heads of States it is not unusual for agreements to be made between Governments. Such agreements, which are usually of a technical or administrative character, are made in the names of the signatory Governments, and signed by representatives of those Governments who do not act under Full Powers issued by the Heads of the States : they are not ratified by the Heads of the States, though in some cases some form of acceptance or confirmation by the Governments concerned is employed. As regards agreements of this nature the existing practice should be continued, but before entering on negotiations the Governments of the Empire should consider whether the interests of any other part of the Empire may be affected, and, if so, steps should be taken to ensure that the Government of such part is informed of the proposed negotiations in order that it may have an opportunity of expressing its views.

The Resolution was submitted to the full Conference and unanimously approved. It was thought, however, that it would be of assistance to add a short explanatory statement in connexion with part I (3), setting out the existing procedure in relation to the ratification of Treaties. This procedure is as follows :

(*a*) The ratification of treaties imposing obligations on one part of the Empire is effected at the instance of the Government of that part :

(*b*) The ratification of treaties imposing obligations on more than one part of the Empire is effected after consultation between the Governments of those parts of the Empire concerned. It is for each Government to decide whether Parliamentary approval or legislation is required before desire for, or concurrence in, ratification is intimated by that Government.[1]

At the Imperial Conference of 1926 the Inter-Imperial Relations Committee, in a report which was unanimously adopted by the Conference on the 19th November, commended the Resolution of 1923, which has been quoted above, but added that ' it seemed desirable to examine the working of that Resolution during the past three years and also to consider whether the principles laid down with regard to treaties could not be applied with advantage in a wider sphere '. They went on to report as follows : [2]

[1] *Imperial Conference of 1923 : Summary of Proceedings (Cmd.* 1987 of 1923), p. 15.   [2] *Cmd.* 2768 of 1926, pp. 21–4.

(a) *Procedure in Relation to Treaties.*

We appointed a special Sub-Committee under the Chairmanship of the Minister of Justice of Canada (the Honourable E. Lapointe, K.C.) to consider the question of treaty procedure.

The Sub-Committee, on whose report the following paragraphs are based, found that the Resolution of the Conference of 1923 embodied on most points useful rules for the guidance of the Governments. As they became more thoroughly understood and established, they would prove effective in practice.

Some phases of treaty procedure were examined however in greater detail in the light of experience in order to consider to what extent the Resolution of 1923 might with advantage be supplemented.

Negotiation.

It was agreed in 1923 that any of the Governments of the Empire contemplating the negotiation of a treaty should give due consideration to its possible effect upon other Governments and should take steps to inform Governments likely to be interested of its intention.

This rule should be understood as applying to any negotiations which any Government intends to conduct, so as to leave it to the other Governments to say whether they are likely to be interested.

When a Government has received information of the intention of any other Government to conduct negotiations, it is incumbent upon it to indicate its attitude with reasonable promptitude. So long as the initiating Government receives no adverse comments and so long as its policy involves no active obligations on the part of the other Governments, it may proceed on the assumption that its policy is generally acceptable. It must, however, before taking any steps which might involve the other Governments in any active obligations, obtain their definite assent.

Where by the nature of the treaty it is desirable that it should be ratified on behalf of all the Governments of the Empire, the initiating Government may assume that a Government, which has had full opportunity of indicating its attitude and has made no adverse comments, will concur in the ratification of the treaty. In the case of a Government that prefers not to concur in the ratification of a treaty unless it has been signed by a plenipotentiary authorized to act on its behalf, it will advise the appointment of a plenipotentiary so to act.

Form of Treaty.

Some treaties begin with a list of the contracting countries and not with a list of Heads of States. In the case of treaties negotiated under the auspices of the League of Nations, adherence to the wording of the Annex to the Covenant for the purpose of describing the contracting party has led to the use in the preamble of the term ' British Empire ' with an enumeration of the Dominions and India if parties to the Convention but without any mention of Great Britain and Northern Ireland and the Colonies and Protectorates. These are only included by virtue of their being covered by the term ' British Empire '. This practice, while suggesting that the Dominions and India are not on a footing of equality with Great Britain as participants in the treaties in question, tends to obscurity and misunderstanding and is generally unsatisfactory.

As a means of overcoming this difficulty it is recommended that all treaties (other than agreements between Governments) whether negoti-ated under the auspices of the League or not should be made in the name of Heads of States, and, if the treaty is signed on behalf of any or all of the Governments of the Empire, the treaty should be made in the name of the King as the symbol of the special relationship between the different parts of the Empire. The British units on behalf of which the treaty is signed should be grouped together in the following order : Great Britain and Northern Ireland and all parts of the British Empire which are not separate members of the League, Canada, Australia, New Zealand, South Africa, Irish Free State, India. A specimen form of treaty as recommended is attached as an appendix to the Committee's Report.

In the case of a treaty applying to only one part of the Empire it should be stated to be made by the King on behalf of that part.

The making of the treaty in the name of the King as the symbol of the special relationship between the different parts of the Empire will render superfluous the inclusion of any provision that its terms must not be regarded as regulating *inter se* the rights and obligations of the various territories on behalf of which it has been signed in the name of the King. In this connexion it must be borne in mind that the question was discussed at the Arms Traffic Conference in 1925, and that the Legal Committee of that Conference laid it down that the principle to which the foregoing sentence gives expression underlies all international conventions.

In the case of some international agreements the Governments of different parts of the Empire may be willing to apply between them-selves some of the provisions as an administrative measure. In this case they should state the extent to which and the terms on which such provisions are to apply. Where international agreements are to be applied between the different parts of the Empire, the form of a treaty between Heads of States should be avoided.

Full Powers.

The plenipotentiaries for the various British units should have Full Powers, issued in each case by the King on the advice of the Government concerned, indicating and corresponding to the part of the Empire for which they are to sign. It will frequently be found convenient, par-ticularly where there are some parts of the Empire on which it is not contemplated that active obligations will be imposed, but where the position of the British subjects belonging to these parts will be affected, for such Government to advise the issue of Full Powers on their behalf to the plenipotentiary appointed to act on behalf of the Government or Governments mainly concerned. In other cases provision might be made for accession by other parts of the Empire at a later date.

Signature.

In the cases where the names of countries are appended to the signa-tures in a treaty, the different parts of the Empire should be designated in the same manner as is proposed in regard to the list of plenipotentiaries in the preamble to the treaty. The signatures of the plenipotentiaries of the various parts of the Empire should be grouped together in the same order as is proposed above.

The signature of a treaty on behalf of a part of the Empire should cover territories for which a mandate has been given to that part of the Empire, unless the contrary is stated at the time of the signature.

Coming into force of Multilateral Treaties.

In general, treaties contain a ratification clause and a provision that the treaty will come into force on the deposit of a certain number of ratifications. The question has sometimes arisen in connexion with treaties negotiated under the auspices of the League whether, for the purpose of making up the number of ratifications necessary to bring the treaty into force, ratifications on behalf of different parts of the Empire which are separate Members of the League should be counted as separate ratifications. In order to avoid any difficulty in future, it is recommended that, when it is thought necessary that a treaty should contain a clause of this character, it should take the form of a provision that the treaty should come into force when it has been ratified on behalf of so many separate Members of the League.

We think that some convenient opportunity should be taken of explaining to the other Members of the League the changes which it is desired to make in the form of treaties and the reasons for which they are desired. We should also recommend that the various Governments of the Empire should make it an instruction to their representatives at International Conferences to be held in future that they should use their best endeavours to secure that effect is given to the recommendations contained in the foregoing paragraphs.

One of the recommendations submitted in the last-quoted paragraph was carried out on the 9th March, 1927, when the following statement was made to his colleagues on the Council of the League by Sir Austen Chamberlain :

I understand that a conference under the auspices of the League may assemble in Geneva in July next, and I think it may be convenient to my colleagues to know that at the meeting of the Imperial Conference in London last autumn it was found that, for constitutional reasons with which I need not trouble the Council, the acceptance by the Governments of the British Empire of treaties negotiated under the auspices of the League would be facilitated if a change could be made in the form in which such instruments are drawn up. It has been the practice for League treaties to be made in the form of treaties between states. The common practice before the Treaty of Versailles was for treaties or conventions to be made in the form of an agreement between the heads of states. The Governments of the British Empire hope that instead of continuing the novel form adopted for the first time in the Treaty of Versailles future treaties concluded under the auspices of the League may be made to conform to the general practice followed in the case of other treaties and may be expressed as an agreement between heads of states.

I should add that I made this statement at the express desire of all the Governments represented at the Imperial Conference.

I wish to repeat that we suggest this reversion to the older form because our discussions showed that it will facilitate acceptance of such treaties by the Governments of the British Empire and thus help forward the work of the League.

The Covenant of the League of Nations has omitted to take note of the fact that there is an entity Great Britain as well as the Dominions. The seat which I occupy here and in the Assembly is attributed by the Covenant to the 'British Empire', but the Dominions sit in the Assembly in their own names. Great Britain appears nowhere, and the existing form of treaty concluded under the auspices of the League, therefore, causes us some inconvenience. If the League were willing to revert to the older and well-established form, it would facilitate our acceptance of treaties negotiated under its auspices.

The Council took note of this statement, and the Secretariat of the League appears thereafter to have followed the procedure desired.

APPENDIX

Frontier Relations between Canada and the United States

(a) WATER QUESTIONS ARISING IN THE BASIN OF THE ST. LAWRENCE AND THE GREAT LAKES.[1]

IN the text of this book, mention has already been made [2] of the Washington Treaty of the 11th January, 1909, which dealt with boundary waters and questions arising along the boundary between Canada and the United States by setting up a body known as the International Joint Commission. It has also been mentioned that during the first sixteen years of its existence this Commission had made several investigations into particular problems relating to power, levels, and navigation in the Basin of the St. Lawrence and the Great Lakes. By the year 1928 the whole complex of water problems arising in this Basin was in a fair way to being taken in hand and solved as a unity by co-operation between the two countries between whom the sovereignty over these waters and their shores was divided; and an expert of such high authority as Mr. Herbert Hoover did not hesitate to speak of this as 'the greatest engineering project of modern history.' [3]

For laymen this project had a double interest. It illustrated the command which modern Western Man had acquired over physical nature; and at the same time it illustrated the power of Nature, as the arbitress of Man's economic activities, to override his political dispositions.

On the first point, it is sufficient to mention that the Sanitary District of Chicago, in wrestling with the problem of getting rid of its sewage without contaminating its water-supply, had hit upon the expedient of diverting the water of the Great Lakes into the Mississippi System in such volume as to lower the average water level in the Basin of the Great Lakes and the St. Lawrence appreciably within the first quarter of the twentieth century.[4] This stupendous drain was proving a serious impediment to water transport on the Great Lakes, and, together with the diversion of water from the Niagara River for the generation of power, it was incidentally threatening to change the face and mar the beauty of the Niagara Falls.[5]

The way in which the economic unity of the Basin cut across the political division between Canada and the United States was constantly being brought out while these great water questions were under consideration. For example, the action of the Chicago Sanitary District in diverting

[1] See H. Lawrence: 'Waterways Problems on the Canadian Boundary' in *Foreign Affairs: An American Quarterly Review*, July 1926.

[2] See Section (iv) (a) above.

[3] Address delivered on the 12th March, 1927, to the New Haven (Conn.) Chamber of Commerce (reported in *The United States Daily*, 14th March, 1927).

[4] Lawrence, *op. cit.*, p. 565. Chicago sought to prove that five-sixths of the total fall of two and a half feet was due to other causes than the Sanitary District's operations (see *op. cit.*, p. 572). In a note addressed on the 7th December, 1926, to the British chargé d'affaires at Washington, the U.S. Secretary of State submitted that the opinion, in this sense, of the Chicago Sanitary District's consulting engineers was supported by the report of the Canadian-United States Joint Board of Engineers (for this Board and its report, see pp. 114–15 below).   [5] Lawrence, *op. cit.*, pp. 564–5.

the water of the Great Lakes into the Mississippi System led to a controversy in which Chicago City and Illinois State were ranged on one side and almost all the other riverain cities and states of the United States, as well as the Dominion of Canada, on the other. Diplomatic correspondence between the Federal and the Royal Governments and legal proceedings in the Supreme Court of the United States between the Federal Government and the Sanitary District of Chicago went on concurrently. It should be added that both sets of proceedings were remarkably dilatory. The first representations by the Canadian Government seem to have been made in 1912;[1] in 1926, correspondence on the subject was reopened by Canada through the channel of the British Embassy at Washington;[2] but by the spring of 1928 little had been achieved beyond an agreement that the correspondence which had passed up to date should be published.[3] In his notes of the 26th July, 1926, and the 17th October, 1927, the U.S. Secretary of State deprecated entering into a diplomatic discussion of the legal question in view of the fact that the issues involved in certain cases which were pending in the Supreme Court of the United States were closely parallel to the questions presented in the British and Canadian notes. The legal proceedings here referred to had been instituted originally, before a less exalted tribunal, as far back as the year 1908; yet the case was still being heard by the Supreme Court in April 1928.

Again, various schemes for the generation of water power gave rise to controversies which were primarily domestic. In Canada, the Province of Quebec, as represented by the Prime Minister of the Provincial Government, Mr. Taschereau, took a strong line—on the strength of a decision, rendered by the Privy Council in London, which was interpreted as establishing the principle that the bed of the St. Lawrence belonged to the Province, and not to the Dominion, in so far as it lay within the territory of the Province. Mr. Taschereau demanded an embargo on the export of power from Canada to the United States, and he looked with some disfavour upon the St. Lawrence waterway scheme, on the ground that it would involve the Dominion, and *pro rata* the Province, in a burden of debt for a purpose which might actually prove detrimental to the interest of the port of Montreal.[4] In taking this line, Mr. Taschereau bid for, and

[1] Lawrence, *op. cit.*

[2] For the debate of the 25th March, 1926, in the Canadian Parliament, in which the Canadian Government was called upon to reopen the question, see *The Times*, 26th March, 1926.

[3] See *The United States Daily*, 20th April, 1928, for texts of a note of the 5th February, 1926, from the British Ambassador at Washington to the United States Secretary of State, and a note of the 28th April, 1926, from the British chargé d'affaires at Washington; *The United States Daily*, 21st April, 1928, for the texts of Note No. 299 (undated) from the British chargé d'affaires at Washington, and a note of the 26th July, 1926, from Mr. Kellogg; a note of the 16th November, 1926, from the British chargé d'affaires, and a note of the 17th December, 1926, from Mr. Kellogg; and *The United States Daily*, 23rd April, 1928, for texts of a note of the 1st September, 1927, from the Canadian chargé d'affaires at Washington and a note of the 17th October, 1927, from the U.S. Secretary of State.

[4] For Mr. Taschereau's policy, see *The Times*, 15th January and 28th November, 1925; 14th January, 1926; 21st January, 1927. Compare a memorial, made public on the 10th March, 1926, from the Merchants' Association of New York State to President Coolidge. In this memorial (as reported in *The New York Times*, 11th March, 1926) it was contended, on the showing of certain legal decisions, that the bed of the St. Lawrence along the New York frontage of the river, up to the international boundary, was the property of New York State and not of the United States.

obtained, the support of his *confrère* Mr. Ferguson, the Prime Minister of Ontario.[1] On the other hand, the prairie provinces of the Dominion looked at the question from the same angle as the Middle Western States of the United States, since inland districts whose prosperity depended upon the export of agricultural produce, on whichever side of the frontier they might happen to lie, could not fail to be attracted by a waterway scheme which promised to bring ocean-going vessels to the lake ports.

Again, the New York State Water Power Commission seems to have succeeded in arriving at an understanding with the corresponding authorities in the Canadian Province of Ontario for the generation of water power from the St. Lawrence on the principle of an equal division of benefit between the parties; and on the basis of this understanding the Commission proceeded to enter into treaty with private enterprises for the actual development of the potential power in this sector when Governor Smith of New York State intervened and compelled the Commission to suspend these proceedings.[2]

These were some examples of the tendency for controversy over the problem of the Great Lakes and St. Lawrence Basin to align itself on other than national lines; but perhaps the most striking illustrations are to be found in the disputes over the fundamental question of the route which the proposed thoroughfare from the Great Lakes to the Atlantic was to follow. There were three principal schemes in the field: one from Georgian Bay on Lake Huron to the St. Lawrence at Montreal; another from either Oswego on Lake Ontario or Buffalo on Lake Erie to the Hudson at Troy; and a third following as closely as possible the natural drainage line of the Basin, first through the chain of the Lakes and then down the course of the St. Lawrence, with loop canals at the various falls and rapids. In terms of political geography, the first of these schemes was 'all Canadian', the second (in its longer and more costly form, in which the canal was to take off at Buffalo) was 'all United States', and the third was international. Yet the advocacy of these alternatives was not determined by political allegiances. The cities of Montreal and New York, which were at present the heads of navigation for the two ocean routes that came within closest range of the Great Lakes, were both inclined to be hostile to any scheme whatsoever, on the calculation that their prosperity would suffer if they were 'side-tracked' or even if, while remaining on the route, they were reduced to being ports of call instead of terminals.[3] On this question, as has been mentioned already, the cleavage was not between Canada and the United States but between the eastern parts of both countries on the one hand and the middle-western parts on the other; and, as far as the United States was concerned, this fact was illustrated by an altercation which arose in March 1926 at Washington. The Secretary of War and the Secretary of the Navy gave public expression to the view that, for strategic reasons, any waterways connecting the Great Lakes with the Atlantic

[1] See *The Times*, 15th January, 1925; 14th January and 6th October, 1926; 1st May, 1928.
[2] See *The New York Times*, 25th September and 9th December, 1926.
[3] See Lawrence, *op. cit.*, pp. 560–2, and *The Times*, 17th April, 1928. Mr. Dempsey, the Chairman of the Rivers and Harbours Committee of the House of Representatives at Washington, who was one of the leading advocates in the United States of the Hudson route as opposed to the St. Lawrence route, did not omit to make capital out of the attitude assumed by Mr. Taschereau (see *The Times*, 13th January, 1926).

I

Seaboard ought to be constructed entirely within United States territory; whereupon the advocates in the United States of the St. Lawrence route organized a delegation to President Coolidge and published a protest in which they declared that an attempt was being made to sacrifice national interests to local interests and indicted the Secretary of War in the following terms:

For more than a century the United States and Canada have had 3,000 miles of unguarded boundary line—not a soldier, not a gun, not a suspicion, not a fear—and now the Secretary of War raises the question of defense. One hundred years of peace between Canada and the United States, of unguarded boundary lines between two great nations—this a world wonder and a world example—is now to be broken or jeopardized merely to defeat 40,000,000 landlocked people in their natural desire to use the St. Lawrence as a way out to the sea.[1]

It remains to record, very briefly, the course of the negotiations and investigations concerning the Great Lakes and St. Lawrence Project down to June 1928.

'Under arrangements in 1919, between the United States and Canada, the International Joint Commission made an investigation of river improvement between Montreal and Lake Ontario, setting out its conclusions and recommendations in a report under date of January 6, 1922. That commission strongly endorsed the plan for the improvement of the St. Lawrence River and recommended that before the project should be actually undertaken, the engineering features should receive "that further and complete study that its magnitude and importance demand".' [2]

On the 14th March, 1924, the United States Government appointed a United States St. Lawrence Commission under the chairmanship of the Secretary of Commerce, Mr. Herbert Hoover; on the 7th May, 1924, the Canadian Government appointed a corresponding body under the title of the National Advisory Committee of Canada; and thereafter the two Governments, in accordance with one of the recommendations in the International Joint Commission's report, agreed, in an exchange of notes dated the 14th February and the 17th March, 1925, to set up a Joint Board of three United States and three Canadian engineers to make an exhaustive expert investigation.[3] The United States Government consented that the question of the diversion of water from the Great Lakes Basin by the Sanitary District of Chicago should be included in the engineers' terms of reference; [4] and in February 1926 it was said to view with favour the negotiation of an agreement with Canada to cover the entire group of related questions concerning the joint use of the Great Lakes and the St. Lawrence by the two countries. According to this statement, it was contemplated that such agreement should deal with the three following matters: first, a through-route via the St. Lawrence for ocean-going vessels, with an incidental development of water power; second, lake levels; and third, the preservation of Niagara Falls.[5] On the 16th November, 1926,

[1] *The New York Times*, 11th March, 1926.
[2] Report to President Coolidge from the Chairman of the United States St. Lawrence Commission, Mr. Herbert Hoover, published in *The United States Daily*, 3rd January, 1927.
[3] Hoover, *op. cit.*; Lawrence, *op. cit.*, p. 562; see also Mr. Kellogg's note of the 13th April, 1927, published in *The United States Daily*, 16th July, 1927.
[4] *The New York Times*, 25th February, 1926.
[5] For this statement, see *The New York Times*, *loc. cit.*

the Joint Board of Engineers presented a report [1] which was comprehensive but not unanimous or conclusive.[2] Nevertheless, on the strength of it, Mr. Hoover, as Chairman of the United States St. Lawrence Commission, presented a report of his own to President Coolidge at the beginning of the year 1927 in which he drew attention to the growing urgency for the Middle West of cheaper communication with the ocean, declared in favour of the St. Lawrence as against the Hudson route, argued that the financial problem could be overcome by the incidental generation and sale of power, and summed up the conclusions of the Commission as follows:

First: The construction of the shipway from the Great Lakes to the sea is imperative both for the relief and for the future development of a vast area in the interior of the continent.

Second: The shipway should be constructed on the St. Lawrence route, provided suitable agreement can be made for its joint undertaking with the Dominion of Canada.

Third: That the development of the power resources of the St. Lawrence should be undertaken by appropriate agencies.

Fourth: That negotiations should be entered into with Canada in an endeavour to arrive at an agreement upon all these subjects. In such negotiations the United States should recognize the proper relations of New York to the power development in the International Section.

Mr. Hoover followed up this report in an address [3] delivered on the 12th March, 1927, to the New Haven (Conn.) Chamber of Commerce. On this occasion he sought to allay certain Canadian anxieties by the following declaration:

It has been suggested by someone that if we jointly undertake to construct this great enterprise it would imply joint American control with Canada over the Canadian territory and that such joint control would be repugnant to the Canadian sense of independence. I may say at once that it would be equally repugnant to the American people, and no such suggestion has ever come from the American side. Our existing improvements along this whole water highway do not, nor have they ever implied, such an invasion.

At the same time, he made the following recommendation:

I would suggest that all these problems would be much simplified if we were to establish some sort of joint governmental body in the nature of a St. Lawrence Corporation or Authority whose personnel would be chosen by the two Governments, whose bonds would be mutually guaranteed by the two Governments and to whom would be entrusted the job of carrying through the project. The finance could thus be secured at the lowest rates in the world and many difficult questions could be dissolved by administrative methods.

On the 13th April, 1927, the U.S. Secretary of State, Mr. Kellogg, addressed a note [4] to the Canadian Minister at Washington, Mr. Massey, in which he followed Mr. Hoover in emphasising the amount of agreement in

[1] Text in *The United States Daily*, 3rd January, 1927.
[2] See *The Times*, 25th November, 1926.
[3] Text in *The United States Daily*, 14th March, 1927.
[4] Text in *ibid.*, 16th July, 1927. The relevant correspondence between the Federal and the Dominion Government, from the 13th April, 1927, to the 7th April, 1928, inclusive, is printed in the Canadian White Paper, *St. Lawrence Waterway Project* (Ottawa, 1928).

the Engineers' Report, announced that the United States Government adopted the recommendations of Mr. Hoover's Commission, and suggested that the two Governments should enter into negotiations for a convention on the subject. The Canadian Prime Minister replied [1] by emphasizing the differences of opinion in the Engineers' Report, noting that the appendices to the Report were not yet completed, and mentioning that the Canadian National Advisory Committee had not yet reported on its part. Meanwhile public opinion on the matter in Canada seems to have been slower to crystallize than it had been in the United States,[2] and the National Advisory Committee did not report until the 11th January, 1928.[3] The presentation of their report gave rise to a discussion in the Canadian Senate, in which Senator G. P. Graham, the former Chairman of the National Advisory Committee, deprecated proceeding with the project too precipitately, while Senator W. L. McDougald, the chairman of the Montreal Harbour Commission, submitted, as the considered opinion of himself, in his official capacity, and of his technical staff, that the completion of the project would not diminish but would greatly increase the prosperity of Montreal. Senator McDougald also drew attention to the immense possibilities of increasing the population and wealth of the Dominion which were implicit in the plans for incidental development of water-power.[4] Meanwhile the Canadian National Advisory Committee's report had been communicated by the Canadian Government to the United States Government on the 31st January, 1928; and a fresh diplomatic correspondence followed.[5] On the 12th March Mr. Kellogg suggested the appointment of Commissioners to discuss the question in concrete terms with a view to drawing up an agreement. On the 5th April the Dominion Government drew attention to the difficulty of reconciling the proposal to finance the waterway project by the incidental development of water power with 'the fact that the market for hydro-electric power in Canada, though large and rapidly expanding,' had 'definitive limitations,' and 'that export of power' was 'considered contrary to public policy'. In the same note, the Dominion Government expressed the wish to clear up the situation as between itself and the Provincial Governments of Quebec and Ontario before carrying its discussions with the United States Government a stage farther.[6] On the 7th April Mr. Kellogg acknowledged this note and at the same time suggested that the initiation of negotiations for a treaty between the two countries need not be postponed.

On the 7th June, 1928, the Dominion Minister of Public Works announced that the Government had decided, subject to an arrangement with the United States about the work to be done on the St. Lawrence Channel, to establish the Great Lakes terminal at Prescott in Eastern Ontario; and the House of Commons at Ottawa passed a vote of $1,500,000

---

[1] Text of his reply in *The United States Daily, loc. cit.*

[2] For public opinion in Canada see *The Times,* 4th January, 1927.

[3] See *ibid.,* 7th and 11th January, 1928. Text of the Report in the Canadian White Paper, *St. Lawrence Waterway Project* (Ottawa, 1928).

[4] See the *Shipping Register* of Montreal, 4th February, 1928.

[5] Texts of this correspondence in *The United States Daily,* 18th April, 1928; cf. *The Times,* 17th April, 1928.

[6] See the Canadian White Paper, *St. Lawrence Waterway Project* (Ottawa, 1928) for the texts of Orders in Council referring to the Supreme Court of Canada certain questions as to water-power rights of the Dominion and the Provinces.

£300,000), the initial part of the contemplated expenditure of $4,000,000 (£800,000) on docks and transhipment facilities.[1]

This was the point which had been reached at the moment when the present volume went to press.

(b) THE SMUGGLING PROBLEM.

The introduction, in the United States, of a complete and universal ban upon alcoholic liquors in the year 1919, while prohibition remained partial and local in Canada, led inevitably to smuggling across the Canadian-United States frontier on a large scale; and the efforts of the United States authorities to put a stop to this illicit traffic led in turn to 'incidents' of a kind which, for more than a century, had been almost unknown along this traditionally peaceful border.[2]

In May 1925 the United States Customs Guards along the Canadian border were reinforced,[3] and in June 1927 further measures for making the control along this border more effective were considered by the United States authorities.[4]

Meanwhile the Canadian Government gave practical proofs of its desire to act as a good neighbour towards the United States Government over this new frontier problem.

On the 6th June, 1924, for example, there was signed at Washington a convention[5] between Canada and the United States to aid in suppressing smuggling operations along the border and in the arrest and prosecution of persons violating the narcotic laws of either Government; and on the 8th January, 1925, a supplementary convention[6] to provide for extradition on account of crimes or offences committed against the laws for the suppression of the traffic in narcotics. Ratifications of both these instruments were exchanged on the 17th July, 1925.

The smuggling of drugs was, of course, a traffic which both Governments were equally concerned to suppress; but Canada also took measures to assist the United States in enforcing the special United States legislation regarding alcoholic liquors.

The profits of smuggling liquor from Canada into the United States were so great that the smugglers could afford to pay heavy overhead charges; and accordingly the Canadian Customs Service was exposed to temptations of corruption which seem to have had a demoralizing effect upon some of its members. This threatened not only to make trouble in Canada's foreign relations with her great neighbour but to lower the standards of Canadian public life, and the 'Customs Scandals' became a prominent issue in Canadian home affairs.[7] To trace the influence of that issue upon the

---

[1] *The Times*, 8th June, 1928.

[2] For characteristic examples of such incidents see *The Times*, 7th June and 17th December, 1924; 22nd February and 2nd October, 1926. One of these incidents gave rise to a discussion in the House of Commons at Ottawa on the 24th April, 1928 (*The Times*, 26th April, 1928), and a note on the subject was addressed on the 28th April, 1928, by the Canadian Minister at Washington to the State Department. (Text of this note in *The United States Daily*, 30th April, 1928).

[3] *The Times*, 16th May, 1925.　　　　[4] *The United States Daily*, 4th June, 1927.

[5] Text in British Parliamentary Paper *Cmd.* 2512 of 1925.

[6] Text in British Parliamentary Paper *Cmd.* 2513 of 1925.

[7] The material interests of the Dominion Government were also affected, since the 'boot-leggers' recouped themselves for their overhead charges by smuggling return-cargoes

vicissitudes of Canadian party politics is beyond the scope of this Survey. It is sufficient to note that during the year 1926 the state of the Customs Department was investigated by a special parliamentary committee,[1] and that the investigation was continued by a Royal Commission[2] which eventually reported in January 1928.[3]

Meanwhile His Majesty's Government in Great Britain, in an *aide memoire* of the 27th March, 1926,[4] had made a spontaneous and voluntary offer of co-operation with the United States Government for the prevention of liquor smuggling into the United States from the Bahamas; this offer had been accepted by the United States Government on the 26th April, 1926;[5] in July 1926 officials of the two Governments had met in London to discuss the situation in concrete terms and had reported on the 27th of the month;[6] and on the 29th September, 1926, His Majesty's Government in Great Britain had informed the United States Government that it considered the suggestions made at the London Conference to be operative as from that date.[7] This arrangement paved the way for similar co-operation between the Canadian Government and the United States Government.[8] On the 28th December, 1926, the Canadian Minister of Customs declared that he intended to give full effect to the anti-smuggling convention with the United States, particularly in the matter of the illegal export of liquor, and at the same time he announced that a cargo of liquor on a ship at Victoria, British Columbia, had been seized because the Customs Department had proof that the cargo was not going to the port in Mexico for which clearance papers had been taken out.[9] A conference between the Canadian Royal Commission on Customs and Excise and certain United States officials, to discuss the smuggling problem along the Canadian-United States border, was held in Washington on the 29th and 30th August, 1927.[10]

The problem proved difficult to solve, because the incentive for smuggling was so strong and the length of the frontier so great. Statistics published at the beginning of the year 1927 showed that, since the adoption of the Volstead Act in the United States on the 29th January, 1919, liquor shipments from Canada to the United States had increased until the value of the beer and ale imported annually into the United States from Canada had risen to $6,000,000 (approximately £1,200,000) and the value of the whisky to $15,000,000 (approximately £3,000,000). The statistics also showed that, in spite of the anti-smuggling convention, the value of liquor shipments had increased in the year 1926 by $5,000,000 (approximately

of valuable merchandise (silks, jewellery, &c.) into Canada. The consequent loss of revenue to the Government was appreciable, while private Canadian business interests also stood to suffer from the competition of smuggled goods.

[1] See *The New York Times*, 20th June, 1926; *The Times*, 20th December, 1926.
[2] *The Manchester Guardian*, 6th January, 1927.
[3] *The Times*, 30th January, 1928.
[4] Text in *The United States Daily*, 2nd March, 1927.
[5] Text of Mr. Kellogg's note of the 26th April, 1926, in *The United States Daily*, 3rd March, 1927.
[6] Text of this report in *The United States Daily, loc. cit.*
[7] *The United States Daily, loc. cit.*
[8] See *The New York Times*, 19th and 20th August, 1926.
[9] *The Times* and *The New York Times*, 29th December, 1926.
[10] Text of the official summary of the minutes of this Conference in *The United States Daily*, 7th and 8th February, 1928.

£1,000,000).[1] Again, in 1927, according to evidence taken from Canadian customs officials by the Canadian Royal Commission, 91 per cent. of the alcoholic beverages exported from Canada went to the United States.[2] These figures indicated the magnitude of the problem; but the good relations which had been established in regard to it between the two Governments concerned made it probable that the problem would be solved and virtually certain that its existence would not have an untoward effect upon those conditions of peace and goodwill which had been happily prevalent along the Canadian-United States border for more than a century.

[1] For these statistics see *The Times*, 14th January, 1927.
[2] *The United States Daily*, 8th February, 1928.

INDEX

Abyssinia, 19.

Aden, 8.

Afghanistan, 4 *n.*; Afghan War, 46 *n.*

Africa, British East, 41.

—, French West, 86.

—, South, accessibility of increased, 8; Afrikanders, 37 *n.*; British Empire, relations with, 20–3; Dominion Status, 4 *n.*, 28, 29 *n.*, 38 *n.*, 39, 68; Great Britain, representation of in, 81, 82; Indians in, 13; Lausanne Treaty ratified, 90; mandate for SW. Africa, 61; Muslims in, 6; South Africans of English descent, 21; Transvaal Nationalists, 21; 'White South Africa', 41. *See also under* British Empire; Dominions; Hertzog, General Hon. J. B. M.; League of Nations; Smuts, Rt. Hon. J. C.

—, South-West, 61.

Algeria, 86.

America, Latin, 9.

Amery, the Rt. Hon. L. S., 19, 79, 80, 82, 83.

'Anzacs', 48, 50.

Argentine, immigration into, 11.

Arms Traffic Conference, 1925, 56, 108.

Assyrian Christians, 7.

Australia, Catholics in, 6; development of, 40; Dominion Status, 4 *n.*, 68; and General War, 33; immigration into, 11, 12; Lausanne Treaty ratified, 90; liaison officer from in London, 78, 81; mandate for New Guinea, 61; and security in the Pacific, 11; United States—influence of in, 41 *n.*;—diplomatic representation between, 70–1. *See also under* British Empire; Bruce, Rt. Hon. S. M.; Chanāq Incident; Dominions; Hughes, Rt. Hon. W. M.; League of Nations; Nauru.

Austria, 57 *n.*

Baldwin, Rt. Hon. Stanley, 61.

Balfour, Lord, 1, 85.

Balfour Declaration of 1917, 6.

Bali, island of, 5.

Bavaria, 36 *n.*

Belgium, 18 *n.*, 60 *n.*

Belligerency, 'passive' and 'active', 2–3, 23–4, 46–52.

Bennett, Mr. R. B., 67.

Black Sea Straits, 47.

Borden, Sir Robert, 17 *n.*, 23 *n.*, 66 *n.*; member of British Empire delegation at Peace Conference, 72–3; on British Empire representation at Peace Conference, 83–4, 85; on Canadian representation at Peace Conference, 104.

Bourassa, Mr. J. H. N., 82.

Brazil, 41, 59; immigration into, 11.

British Commonwealth of Nations. *See under* British Empire.

British Empire:

British Commonwealth of Nations, evolution of, 16, 39, 40; relations of with League of Nations, 24, 44; resemblances of to League of Nations, 18–24, 27; self-government a necessary qualification for membership of, 18–19; 'super-state' incompatible with, 19–20.

Civilizations in, 5–7, 13, 24, 30.

Communications, 8, 11, 80, 81.

Conferences, international, representation of at, 83–99.

Constitution, written, question of, 26, 28.

Consultation between constituent members of, Mr. MacDonald's note to Dominions regarding (23 June, 1924), 75–6, 78; meeting proposed to discuss note, 76, 79; replies to note—Africa, South, 79;—Australia, 77–8, 79, 80;—Canada, 78–9;—Newfoundland, 78.

Europo-centric system, no longer a part of, 30–3.

Extent of the, 4.

Geneva Protocol and, 80.

Mandate for Nauru, 61.

Migration and, 11–13, 24.

Naval strength of, 2.

Outlawry of war and, 23.

Races in, 5.

Religions in, 6.

Security and, 10–11.

State, a single, 1, 3–4.

States, an association of sovereign and independent, 14–15.

Unanimous decision needed for settlement of all questions in, 23.

British Empire—*continued.*
See also under Dominions; Lausanne
Conference; League of Nations;
London Conference; Peace Confer-
ence of Paris; Washington Con-
ference.
Bruce, Rt. Hon. S. M., speech of to
United States Pilgrims' Association at
New York, 29 Dec. 1926, 14 *n.*, 31 *n.*,
33, 37, 40 *n.*; on diplomatic representa-
tion in the United States, 71; on
British Empire in relation to League
of Nations, 27 *n.*; on inadvisability of
written constitution for British Empire,
28.
Buddhism, Hinayana, 6.
Bulgaria, 36 *n.*, 57 *n.*
Burma, 6, 44.

Canada:
Chanāq Incident, controversy in Cana-
dian Parliament regarding, 50-1.
Customs Scandal, 117-18.
Development of, 40.
Dominion Status of, 4 *n.*, 27, 28, 29 *n.*,
39, 67-8.
France, diplomatic representation of
in, 67.
French Canadians, 37, 60 *n.*
Geneva Protocol, attitude to, 58.
Great Britain, agreement with re-
garding diplomatic representation,
20; representation in, 81, 82.
Immigration into, 11, 12.
Japan, diplomatic representation be-
tween, 67.
Nationals of, defined in 1921 Act,
2 *n.*
Permanent Court, attitude of regard-
ing optional clause of statute, 60 *n.*
Security of, 9, 10, 11.
Treaty-making powers of, 104.
United States:
Canadian War Mission at Washing-
ton, 64.
Diplomatic Representation between,
64-7, 70; discussed during 1918-
19, 65; proposal made to Cana-
dian Parliament regarding, May
1920, 65-6, 68; debates on in
Canadian Parliament, 66; Mr.
Massey appointed to Washington,
66; Mr. Phillips appointed to
Ottawa, 66, 100.
Economic relations with, 24.
Frontier between, 9, 61-2.

Halibut fisheries, treaty regarding,
101-4; statement in Parliament
regarding Canadian plenipoten-
tiary's powers to sign, 102; de-
scribed as between Great Britain
and United States, 103; United
States ratification, 103.
Influence of in, 10, 41 *n.*
International Joint Commission set
up, 62-4, 66; cases investigated
by, 63-4, 111, 114; jurisdiction of,
63; treaty regarding 62, 63.
Lake of the Woods convention, 64.
Peace Bridge opened, 61.
St. Lawrence Canal projects, 113-17.
Smuggling problem, 117-19.
Water questions between, 62, 111-
17.
See also under Borden, Sir Robert;
British Empire; Chanāq Incident;
Dominions; Geneva Protocol;
King, Mr. Mackenzie; Lausanne
Conference; Lausanne Treaty;
League of Nations; Sèvres Treaty;
Treaties; United States, immigra-
tion into.
U.S.S.R., debate on rupture with, 82.
Cecil, Lord Robert, 51.
Ceylon, 6, 36, 40, 44.
Chamberlain, Sir Austen, 15 *n.*, 109.
Chanāq Incident of Sept. 1922, 3, 24,
46-52, 85; Great Britain's telegram to
Dominions regarding (15 Sept. 1922),
48, 49 *n.*; replies to Great Britain's
telegram—Africa, South, 50, 51 *n.*;
—Australia, 49;—Canada, 50;—New
Zealand, 49; discussion of in League of
Nations Assembly, 51, 52; question of
referring to League of Nations, 51 *n.*;
Angora Government decides to confer
with Allied Powers, 51; effects of inci-
dent in Canada, 51.
Chicago, sanitary district of, 111-12, 114.
China, 5, 6, 11, 31, 36 *n.*, 42.
Clifford, Captain B. E. H., 82.
'Constitutional Conference', proposed,
26, 35, 76.
Cook, Sir Joseph, 51.
Coolidge, President, 66, 69, 114, 115.
Cuba, 59-60.
Cyprus, 6, 36.

Dandurand, Senator, 58, 60 *n.*
Denison, Sir Hugh, 70.
Denmark, 59.

Dominions, defined, 16; exempted from certain of Great Britain's treaty obligations, 3; lack of political experience of, 14; representation of—at international conferences, 92, 97-8;—at Lausanne Conference, 85;—on League of Nations, 10, 17, 18;—at London Conference, 92-4;—at Peace Conference, 17, 83-4;—at Washington Conference, 84-5; treaty-making powers of, 99, 100-1.

Dominion Status, 15-16, 19, 27, 28, 29, 31, 36, 37, 38.

Ecuador, 4 n.
Egypt, 4, 6, 15.
Estonia, 59.
Exequaturs, issue of to Foreign Consuls in the Dominions, 71.

Falkland Islands, 42.
Ferguson, Mr., 113.
Fisher, Mr. H. A. L., 51.
Fisheries, international controversies regarding, 101-4.
FitzGerald, Mr. Desmond, 53, 55, 58.
Foster, Sir George, 59.
France, colonial empire of, 18 n.; fisheries controversy with British Empire, 101; immigration into, 11; opposes Dominion representation at Lausanne Conference, 86, 96; post-war position of, 32, 33; War, Act for the Organization of the Nation in time of, 43. See also under Canada; Treaties.

Geneva Protocol, 19, 58, 80.
Germany, 11, 19, 32, 97—See also under Reparation.
Graham, Senator G. P., 116.
Great Britain, bound to European continent, 7, 9, 34, 73; Japan, alliance with, 74; migration from, 11, 12; naval supremacy of, 31; representation of Dominions in, 81-3; responsibility of for British Empire, 14; security of, 10, 11; Turkey, Great Britain responsible for British Empire accounts with, 48; U.S.S.R., breaking off of relations with, 82. See also under Africa, South; British Empire; Canada; Chanāq Incident; Lausanne Conference; Lausanne Treaty; Peace Conference of Paris; Sèvres Treaty; Treaties.
Greece, 36 n., 60 n.; war with Turkey, 47 n.

Grey, Lord, 7-8.
Grigg, Sir Edward, 85 n.

Hague Convention (1907), 63.
Hanotaux, M., 51.
Hapsburg Monarchy, 29, 32, 36, 37 n.
Hertzog, General the Hon. J. B. M., on Dominion Status and neutrality, 1 n.; on international status of South Africa, 20; on South African representative in Great Britain, 82; opening speech at Imperial Conference, 1926, 21, 23; speech at Capetown, 13 Dec. 1926, 21; speech at Paarl, 14 Dec. 1926, 22; speech at Pretoria, 20 Dec. 1926, 22.
Hindus, 5.
Hohenzollern Empire, 29, 36.
Hongkong, 5, 42.
Hoover, Mr. Herbert, 111, 114-16.
Howard, Sir Esmé, 68, 69.
Hughes, Rt. Hon. W. M., 6, 26, 35, 49, 102.
Hungary, 36 n., 57 n.

Imām of San'ā, 8.
Imperial Conferences, 53, 74; continuity aimed at in representation at, 78.
—, (1921), 26, 30, 35, 44, 73, 74.
—, (1923), 19, 90, 91, 92, 94, 104, 105-6.
—, (1926), 1, 19, 20-1; Committee on Inter-Imperial Relations, 1, 13, 16, 18, 21, 22, 26, 27, 91 n.; and Dominion Representation, 94-5; and Dominion Representation in U.S., 70-1; and communications and consultation, 80, 81; and treaty-making powers of Dominions, 55-6, 81, 106-9, 110.
Imperial Economic Conference, 1923, 74.
Imperial War Cabinet, 1917 and 1918, 72; Imperial War Conference, 1917, 26, 35.
India, 3, 29 n., 31, 36, 41, 42; emigration from, 11, 44; Government of India Act, 1919, 18, 39; Hinduism in, 13; Islam in, 5-6, 13; ratifies Lausanne Treaty, 90; Parsees in, 6; status of, 18, 39. See also under Africa, South; British Empire; League of Nations.
Industrial Property, international convention regarding protection of, 84.
'Irāq, 4, 6-7, 15. See also under Treaties.
Ireland, anti-Catholic laws in, 38.
Irish Free State, 36, 42, 48; Anglo-Irish Agreement of 1921 regarding, 20, 26-7, 38, 53, 54-6, 66, 67-8, 69; Constitution of, 20, 27; Dominion Status of, 27, 28,

38–9, 54, 67; establishment of, 39, 53; Great Britain—non-participation of in wars undertaken by, 3;—representation of in, 81; migration from, 11; United States—close connexion with 24, 70;—diplomatic representation of in, 20, 66, 67–71, 100. *See also under* British Empire; Lausanne Treaty; League of Nations.

Islamic World, 8, 11, 36 *n.*
Italy, 11, 12, 32, 33, 36 *n.*

Japan, 11, 12, 31, 32, 33, 95. *See also under* Canada; Great Britain.
Jellicoe, Lord, 49.
Jugoslavia, 37 *n.*

Kellogg, Mr., 115, 116.
'Kellogg Pact', 15 *n.*
Kenya, 13, 29 *n.*
King, Mr. Mackenzie, and Chanāq Incident, 48 *n.*, 49 *n.*, 50–2; on diplomatic representation, 82; in France, 67; at London Conference, 92–3, 97; and Lausanne Treaty, 51, 87, 90, 91; at opening of Peace Bridge, 61.

Lapointe, the Hon. E., 101, 102, 103, 107.
Lausanne Conference, Dominion representation at, 85–90, 96, 97, 98; message from Great Britain to Dominion Prime Ministers regarding (27 Oct. 1922), 86; exchange of notes between Great Britain and Canada regarding, 87–9; agreement reached with Canada, 90; Canadian point of view explained at Imperial Conference of 1923, 90.
Lausanne Treaty, 47 *n.*; binding on whole British Empire, 88; ratification of by Canada, 3, 51, 85, 90–2, 104; ratification of by Irish Free State, 90 *n.*; ratification of by India, New Zealand, Australia, and South Africa, 90.
Law, Mr. A. Bonar, 16, 65 *n.*
League of Nations:
  Africa, South, 17.
  Australia, 17.
  British Empire, states members of the, members of the League, 3 *n.*, 10, 17, 18, 52–61.
  Canada, 2 *n.*, 9, 10, 17; elected to non-permanent seat on Council, 53, 59–60. *See also below under* Covenant, Amendment to Art. 10.
  Chanāq Incident and, 51, 52.

  Covenant, Art. 10, Amendment to, Canada's action regarding, 10, 52 *n.*, 56–8; Art. 16, 25; Art. 18, registration of treaties under, 54–5; outlawry of war under, 23, 24, 25.
  India, 17, 18, 52, 53.
  Irish Free State, admission of to, 17, 19, 52, 53–4; candidature of for temporary seat on Council, 20, 58–9; registration of Irish Agreement with League, 54–6.
  Membership, self-government a necessary qualification for, 18–19.
  New Zealand, 17.
  Questionnaire for new members, 54. *See also under* British Empire: British Commonwealth of Nations.
Leeper, Mr. A. W. A., 78, 83.
Lloyd George, Rt. Hon. David, 26, 38, 49, 51 *n.*
Locarno, Pact of, 3.
London Conference (Reparations, 16 July–16 Aug. 1924), Dominion representation at, 92, 93, 94, 96, 97, 98.

Macdonald, Sir John, 100.
Macdonald, Rt. Hon. J. Ramsay, 76, 78, 79, 80, 90 *n.*
McDougald, Senator W. L., 116.
Malaya, British, 6, 8, 40, 44.
Malta, 36, 40.
Mandates, 19, 60–1.
Maskat, 6, 15.
Massey, Mr. Vincent, 66, 115.
Massey, Rt. Hon. W. F., 35.
Meighen, Rt. Hon. A., 26, 52, 74.
Mexico, 4 *n.*, 10. *See also under* United States: immigration.
Migration, 11–13, 19.
Monroe Doctrine, 31.
Montenegro, 37 *n.*
Morocco, 8.
Mudros Armistice, 47 *n.*
Muslims, 5, 8.
Mutual Guarantee, proposed treaty of, 57.

Najd-Hijāz, 4 *n.*
Nansen, Dr., 51.
Nauru, 61.
Naval Disarmament Conference, Three-Power, 61; Dominion representation at, 95, 96.
Nestorian Church, 7.
Netherlands, colonial empire of, 18 *n.*
Netherlands India, 8.

Newfoundland, status of, 4 *n.*, 19; fishing rights of, controversy regarding, 101; representation of in Great Britain, 81. *See also under* United States : immigration.
New Guinea, 61.
New Zealand, development of, 40–1; Dominion status of, 4 *n.*, 68; immigration into, 11, 12; Lausanne Treaty ratified by, 90; mandate for Samoa, 61; representation of in Great Britain, 81, 83; and security in the Pacific, 11. *See also under* British Empire; Chanāq Incident; Dominions; League of Nations; Nauru.
Niagara Falls, 111, 114.
Nichols, Mr. P. B. B., 83.
Nigeria, 6.

Orange Free State, 37 *n.*

Pacific Ocean, the, 8, 11, 31.
Palestine, 6, 15.
Panama Canal, 9.
Papua, status of, 5.
Parsees, 6.
Peace Bridge. *See under* Canada: United States.
Peace Conference of Paris, Dominion Representation at, 17, 23 *n.*, 72, 83–4, 92, 93, 95, 97, 98; no separate representation for Great Britain as apart from British Empire at, 17.
Permanent Court of International Justice, 60 *n.*
Permanent Mandates Commission, 19.
Persia, 58.
Philippines, 8, 36, 42.
Phillips, Mr. William, 66.
Poland, 10, 36 *n.*
Portugal, 60 *n.*

Quebec Act (1774), 38.

Reparation, 2 *n.*, 96, 97. *See also under* London Conference.
Rhodesia, Southern, 4 *n.*, 11, 19, 29 *n.*, 36, 40, 41 *n.*
Rolin, M., 58.
Romanov Empire, 29, 36.
Roos, Mr. Tielman, 21 *n.*
Russia, 42, 46 *n.*; Black Sea Straits, 47–8; Dictatorship in, 36 *n.*; Empire, 32, 33; and League of Nations, 4 *n.*; Muslims in, 6. *See also under* Canada; Great Britain.

Salmond, Sir John, 85 *n.*
Samoa, 61.
San Remo Conference, 86.
Sault Sainte Marie, 64.
Serbia, 37 *n.*
Sèvres Treaty, 47 *n.*, 86, 88; Canadian ratification of, 50, 51; non-ratification of by Great Britain, 51.
Shanghai International Settlement, 42 *n.*
Siam, 6 *n.*, 59.
Singapore, 8.
Smiddy, Professor Timothy, 66, 69.
Smith, Governor, 113.
Smuts, Rt. Hon. J. C., 35, 85 *n.*; on British Empire, 20; and Chanāq Incident, 50; opening speech of at Imperial Conference, 1921, 30, 32, 44, 73.
South Africa. *See under* Africa, South.
Spain, 36 *n.*
Sterling, Mr. F. A., 69.
Straits Settlements, 42.
Successor States, 36, 42.
Sudan, 4, 6.
Suez Canal, 8.

Tascherau, Mr., 112.
Thomas, Mr. J. H., 76, 93, 96–7, 99.
Transvaal, 37 *n.*
Travancore, 7 *n.*
Treaties, bilateral:
   Canada–France (commerce, 29 Jan. 1921), 101.
   Canada–United States (1911), 101; (frontier, and Lake of the Woods, 24 Feb. 1925),·62 *n.*, 64; (halibut fishery, 2 March, 1923), 101–4; (smuggling, 6 June 1924), 117; (extradition, 8 Jan. 1925), 117.
   France–Great Britain (fisheries, 8 April 1904), 101; (guarantee, 28 June 1919), 3.
   Great Britain–'Irāq (10 Oct. 1922), 7.
   Great Britain–United States (Washington, 1871), 100; (Canadian boundary and waterways, 11 Jan. 1909), 62, 63, 64.
'Trucial Chieftainships', 6, 15.
Tunisia, 86.
Turkey, 4 *n.*, 6. *See also under* Chanāq Incident; Great Britain; Greece; Lausanne Treaty; Sèvres Treaty.

United States, 25, 32, 33, 40, 42; immigration into, 11, 12;—restrictions on British immigrants, 2 *n.*, 44;—Canadian immigrants, 45;—Mexico, immigrants from, 45;—Newfoundland, immigrants from, 45;—Immigration Acts (1917), 44; (1921), 45; (1924), 45; and League of Nations, 4 *n.*, 10, 24; liquor smuggling into, 117–19; at Naval Conference, 95; policy of no European commitments, 10; and security in the Pacific, 11, 31; War of Independence, 29. *See also under* Australia; Canada; Irish Free State; Treaties; Versailles Treaty.

Uruguay, 11, 57 *n.*

Versailles Treaty, 2, 17, 18, 73, 92, 109; U.S. non-ratification of, 10.

Vienna, Congress of, 31.

War, outlawry of, 23, 24, 25, 43, 44.

Wales, Prince of, 61.

Washington Conference, 5 *n.*, 74; Dominion representation at, 83–4, 92, 95, 96, 97, 98.

Weihawei, 5 *n.*

Yaman, 4 *n.*, 8.

Yazīdīs, 7.

PRINTED IN ENGLAND AT THE
UNIVERSITY PRESS, OXFORD
BY JOHN JOHNSON
PRINTER TO THE UNIVERSITY